APPRECIATING
ASPERGER
SYNDROME

by the same author

Parenting a Child with Asperger Syndrome
200 Tips and Strategies
Brenda Boyd
ISBN 978 1 84310 137 6

of related interest

Autism Heroes
Portraits of Families Meeting the Challenge
Barbara Firestone, Ph.D.
Forewords by Teddi Cole and Gary Cole and Catherine Lord, Ph.D.
Photographs by Joe Buissink
ISBN 978 1 84310 837 5

The Myriad Gifts of Asperger's Syndrome
John M. Ortiz
ISBN 978 1 84310 883 2

A Self-Determined Future with Asperger Syndrome
Solution Focused Approaches
E. Veronica Bliss and Genevieve Edmonds
Foreword by Bill O'Connell, Director of Training, Focus on Solutions
ISBN 978 1 84310 513 8

APPRECIATING ASPERGER SYNDROME

Looking at the Upside – with 300 Positive Points

BRENDA BOYD

Jessica Kingsley Publishers
London and Philadelphia

First published in 2009
by Jessica Kingsley Publishers
116 Pentonville Road
London N1 9JB, UK
and
400 Market Street, Suite 400
Philadelphia, PA 19106, USA

www.jkp.com

Copyright © Brenda Boyd 2009

Library of Congress Cataloging in Publication Data
A CIP catalog record for this book is available from the Library of Congress

British Library Cataloguing in Publication Data
A CIP catalogue record for this book is available from the British Library

ISBN 978 1 84310 625 8

Printed and bound in the United States by
Thomson-Shore, 7300 Joy Road, Dexter, MI 48130

For my son, Kenneth Hall

ACKNOWLEDGEMENTS

I would like to thank everyone who has helped me along the way – either to understand and appreciate Asperger Syndrome – or to encourage and support me so I could finally get this book written!

Kenneth

Christine and Gerard

Lily and Jim Kennedy

Heather Taylor

Julie Connell

Julie May Noteman

Kate Doherty

Jo Douglas

Dee

And last but not least I would like to think Martin (Bap) Kennedy. Without him, this book would not exist!

CONTENTS

FOREWORD

When my mother asked me to write this foreword, my first reaction was pride. After that, I felt slightly worried - could I do a good enough job, and would it be as difficult to write the Foreword as she had found it to write the book? Certainly, she did find it difficult to write. I can understand that, because although I am positive about AS (I have always said that if they invented a "cure" tomorrow, I would never take it) I could not write an entire book about why AS is a good thing.

My mother could, though. It was very difficult for her, but no great achievement is achieved without great work (unfortunately), and when it comes to this book, I have no doubt that the destination (the book itself) is worth the journey - demanding as that journey may have been.

In a way, it is fitting that this was not an easy book to write. It is an incredibly positive reflection on Aspies that mum had the determination to work so hard, to obsess at times, and to not give up on what would become an excellent book, while many NT's would probably have given up. How apt that a book about appreciating Asperger Syndrome (AS) would, itself, be such a characteristic Asperger's Achievement.

Nor was it a small achievement, but in fact an enormous - and important - one. As mum says in the introduction, "our attitudes are at least as important as our behaviour", and this book serves a great purpose - that of changing our attitudes for the better. It will help parents to be proud of the fact their children have AS, and help the Aspies themselves to be proud of the fact they are Aspies.

In the first chapter, Mum makes a very good extended analogy comparing an Aspie to someone who is visually impaired and walks into lampposts, or steps on toes. It is a remarkably astute one, save for one thing (which she does mention): the fact that, whereas a blind man cannot "learn" to see, an Aspie can - with determination - "learn" social rules. It is helpful that Aspies are so remarkably determined.

When my mum got her own diagnosis, I can honestly say I was not surprised. Although she was very good at creating this fabrication of a fairly normal person, I was able - as someone who knew her and knew about Aspergers - to see through it. Interestingly, the way she felt about my diagnosis was the same way I felt about hers, but now it is becoming increasingly clear that the more she accepts her Aspergers, the more she achieves.

Writing this book, she has done an excellent job of passing that on, and I am certain that many people - myself included - will become more accepting of their own Aspergers, and be able to achieve more in their lives, as a direct result of this book.

Kenneth Hall
Author of Asperger Syndrome,
The Universe and Everything

INTRODUCTION

HOW I REFER TO PEOPLE, USE TERMS ETC.

There are many different names and terms that you can use when you are talking about Asperger Syndrome.

People have different preferences about which terms they like to use, and they can be very sensitive about it. So there is always a risk that using a particular term will cause offence to someone. Obviously that's something I don't want to do. For that reason – and also just to provide a bit of variety – I will use a selection of the usual terms throughout the book to refer to Asperger Syndrome, to people who have been diagnosed with Asperger Syndrome, and to 'typical' people as well (i.e. people who do not have Asperger Syndrome).

Here are some examples of the usual terms that are used when talking about Asperger Syndrome:

- **Aspergers and AS**: These are common abbreviations for Asperger Syndrome.

- **AS person**: A person who has been diagnosed with Asperger Syndrome.

- **ASD**: Autistic Spectrum Disorders, which cover both autism and Asperger Syndrome.

- **Aspie**: A person who has been diagnosed with the condition is sometimes referred to as an AS person or an Aspie.

NT: This is an abbreviation of 'neurotypical' and is sometimes used to refer to people who do not have Asperger Syndrome. People who have not been diagnosed with Asperger Syndrome may therefore be referred to as NT's. (NT suggests that the brain works in a more usual or typical way than is the case in people with Asperger Syndrome.)

I will also use the masculine pronoun when referring to people with Asperger Syndrome, partly because far more males than females are ever diagnosed, and partly for consistency and convenience. Again this is not intended as any disrespect to the many females with the condition.

NO NAMES!

I have made a decision not to say anything in this book that would identify any particular individual. One obvious exception to that is in the case of my son, Kenneth – and he says he does not mind me telling you about him – up to a certain point of course!

It is actually not necessary to identify individual people. One thing I have seen again and again is that there are remarkable similarities between people's experiences. So there is no need to name names.

BACKGROUND TO THE BOOK

'Fools rush in where angels fear to tread.' I'm not sure exactly what that means – but here's what I hope it means. I hope it means that sometimes when you find something really hard to do, and you have to think long and hard before stepping into it, that puts you on the side of the angels rather than on the side of the fools. It would be nice to think that was the case anyway, because I have found this book so hard to write that I have felt very much like a fool at times! Let me tell you a few of the things that were going on before I wrote the book and during the time when I was writing it, and I think you'll understand why.

A book about attitudes

Six years ago or so I wrote *Parenting a Child with Asperger Syndrome: 200 Tips and Strategies*. That was a very different book from this one, because it was a very practical book. This one is not primarily practical – or at least it does not set out to be. It aims to focus on the positive side of Asperger Syndrome – not by brushing the negatives under the carpet, but by trying to understand them and what lies behind them. For the more deeply we understand AS, the more positive we can be. That means that this is really a book about attitudes.

But attitudes can be harder to pin down than behaviour – our own especially – for we are usually better at noticing other people's attitudes than our own. And nobody likes to admit it when their own attitudes are negative. So I had to do a lot of my own inner searching along the way!

Essentially this book will focus on how we think about, understand and appreciate Asperger Syndrome rather than how we manage it. For if I had to name just one thing I have learned in recent years it would be this – our attitudes are at least as important as our actions, and how we think about things has a far greater impact than we realise.

Diagnosis and insight

Up till about ten years ago I had never heard of Asperger Syndrome. Then my son was diagnosed with the condition, and I wanted to find out all about it. But I found it hard to get a handle on what it actually was. On the one hand it seemed that AS was associated with autism. Like autism, it involved an element of impairment in social relationship and interaction. But on the other hand, it also seemed to be linked with types of brilliance and giftedness. Associations were being made between AS and some remarkable people, such as Albert Einstein, Andy Warhol, Beethoven, Hans Christian Anderson, Lewis Carroll, Michaelangelo, Mozart, Vincent Van Gogh and W.B. Yeats (for a fuller discussion of the link between giftedness and AS, see Chapter 10).

Since my son was diagnosed, my life has become immersed in Asperger Syndrome. He was about nine by the time he was diagnosed, but before that, trying to bring him up had been nothing short of a nightmare.

It was a difficult period; and like any Mum in the same position I went through a lot of painful emotions – anxiety, worry, confusion, frustration and anger. I could barely manage his behaviour, and sometimes that made me angry and frustrated – but then nobody else could either, so I was anxious about his future. And a lot of the time he seemed unhappy, so I was very worried about him, and confused. Most of the time though, I was exhausted from trying to sort it all out, and I wasn't sure I knew what I was doing.

When Kenneth was first diagnosed I had mixed feelings, but Kenneth took the news well. He even wrote a book about his experiences as a child with AS, *Asperger Syndrome, the Universe and Everything* (author Kenneth Hall).

There is, incidentally, a funny story behind that which offers a few interesting insights into AS, and gives a good illustration of how people with AS sometimes take things very literally. When the psychologist from the Education Board suggested he should 'write a book', he took her suggestion absolutely seriously, and decided to do exactly that. He had been complaining about how bored he was and she made the suggestion in a light-hearted way. But he assumed, as children with AS often do, that she meant what she said quite literally.

Another insight is one involving the issue of motivation and Asperger Syndrome. It is often said that people with AS (and in particular children) can be very *hard* to motivate, but that is only part of the story. The real truth is that when a person with AS is not interested in something, he can come across as lazy, uncooperative and apathetic.

> It can be extremely hard to discover what might motivate a person with AS, but if the right thing can be found, an Aspie's motivation can be exceptionally high; he can be single-minded, diligent, persistent and even obsessive to an incredibly extreme degree.

Those qualities are very characteristic of people with AS generally; and again they are characteristics that have been associated with some of the world's most remarkable, gifted and innovative and creative people.

Most people, if they are honest about it, do a lot of things because, at least in part, they find it easier and more comfortable to do what the people around them are doing. They conform because they want to fit in. This is a very basic human desire, and it is a bigger motivator for people's behaviour than we realise most of the time.

But it is different for Aspies. By their very nature they are more likely to stand out from the crowd and not fit in. It is hard to tell sometimes whether this is because they have no idea how to fit in, or they don't care whether they fit in or not. (Some Aspies, particularly females, do very much want to fit in and they can learn to do so, or at least seem to do so, by copying what they see around them. This makes them less likely to draw attention to themselves, so it would seem to be more likely that females rather than males will go undiagnosed.)

Kenneth, at the time he wrote the book, was hardly conforming or cooperating in school at all. It was a very big problem. For example, at nine years old he could still see no reason to do handwriting or homework, or any of those 'boring' things that children of that age are expected to do. But for some reason the idea of writing a book interested him and he was motivated to do that. It didn't seem either to occur to him or to bother him that most children don't really write books, or that they really do things like homework.

Aspies are that bit different just by their very nature, which is one of the things that can make them seem eccentric. But who would really want a world without eccentricity? Eccentric people can make life richer and more interesting.

A confession

Kenneth is a young man now, and there has been a lot of water under the bridge in between. In the field of ASD, his book was widely respected. It has helped a lot of people to understand AS from the inside and to view it more positively. But looking back now, there's something I need to admit – if I had been able to find a way to get him through from childhood to manhood without having him diagnosed with AS, I'm pretty sure I would have done it. I don't like to admit that, but it's true.

Like all Mums, I wanted to love and accept my son for exactly who he was, but if I was resistant about accepting the AS 'label' for him, there must have a part of me that was negative about Aspergers. There must have been a part of me that wanted to pretend he was 'normal'. In the end I couldn't – for it became clearer and clearer over time that he needed help; and once the right label had been found, he fitted it incredibly well. (There must, incidentally, be cases similar to his but less obvious or less extreme, where children have Asperger Syndrome but do not get diagnosed.)

A strange duality

Asperger Syndrome has been recognised for about the last 60 years or so, and these days most people have at least heard of it, but there is still a lot of confusion and misunderstanding about what AS actually is. And there is a lot of fascination as well.

Probably the most fascinating thing about Asperger Syndrome is the strange duality whereby it is linked with both autism and giftedness. Both autism and giftedness, as extremes of the human condition, have something fascinating about them. Being linked to both seems to make Asperger Syndrome more fascinating than either.

In reality, however, people who are living with AS are much more likely to see it as a problem condition than a fascinating one. If you are closely involved in the life of someone with AS, or you have been diagnosed with it yourself, you will know at first hand that Asperger Syndrome can be a tough condition to live with. So the truth is that over the last ten years my focus has been on AS problems and trying to find solutions. And when you are focusing so hard on problems, it can make it very hard to be positive.

The missing link

Writing this book has been something of a rubicon for me. Many times while I was writing it things were so difficult personally I felt like giving up. There was a lot going on. For example: (1) I went through a divorce; (2) Kenneth decided that the education system was no longer for him and 'dropped out'; (3) I was diagnosed with clinical depression; (4) there were a lot of changes at work, which in the end I could not cope with, so I resigned; (5) I was finding Kenneth increasingly hard to live with and sent him to live with his Dad.

All of these things made me feel like a fool and a failure at times, and very ill-equipped to write a positive book about Asperger Syndrome. But there is something else that complicated things even more.

About two years ago I got my own diagnosis with Asperger Syndrome, and while I have been writing this book, I have been coming to terms with that. I haven't found it easy, and that in itself made me feel like a hypocrite sometimes, for I had been telling Kenneth for years that he should be proud of who he was. Yet when it came to myself it was a different story.

In the end I came to realise that all my own secret doubts, misgivings and negative feelings were actually important – because they helped me understand attitudes to AS better. As well as that, the process of writing has forced me to face and work through a lot of my own negativity, and I hope I will be able to pass on a lot of what I have observed and learned along the way.

How did I honestly feel about my diagnosis? Well, in some ways I was glad to have it. It helped explain a lot – why I had always secretly felt like such a misfit, for example; why I had never (yet!) found a career that was right for me; and why, by then, I had been divorced three times.

I had gone through various different phases of looking for answers, trying to fit in and be 'normal'. I had thrown myself obsessively into various different approaches to life, religions, philosophies etc.; and I had read a lot about personal development. By the time I got my diagnosis I had spent 17 years in therapy. All these things were part of the path, I suppose, and they had been very helpful, but getting the diagnosis was the pivotal thing.

But in other ways I was negative about the diagnosis. Secretly I had been pretty sure for a long time that I probably had AS too, but despite that I kept on denying it for as long as I could. In the end it took a breakdown to persuade me to go for assessment. Then, even when I found out, I was very wary about telling anyone. Acceptance can be a slow process.

The Asperger advantage?

There is one thing I have found particularly surprising and gratifying about the whole process and it is this.

For a person to deny his (or her) Asperger Syndrome (especially when he knows about the condition and can see it clearly in himself), he must be either (1) a very good actor or (2) cut off from a part of his true identity. For me it turned out to be a bit of both. But I didn't realise that when we cut off one part of ourselves, there may be a high price to pay – for we cannot cut off one part unless we risk losing another. I didn't know what I had lost until I started to find it.

Each person's story is different of course, so can AS be seen as an advantage in a more general way? I would like to answer that question in this book approaching it from three main angles, by trying to:

1. reach a deeper understanding of AS

2. gain some insights into the mysterious link between AS and giftedness

3. suggest ways in which AS (everyday issues and characteristic traits) can be viewed in a more positive way.

IN SUMMARY

For me personally, diagnosis has been a very positive thing. It opened up the door which has allowed me to find out more about who I really was and accept the truth of that. In particular, it has allowed me to unlock aspects of my own creativity that beforehand I had only been dimly aware of (for example story writing, pastel painting and song writing). From a personal point of view, therefore, I can see how it can be an advantage to accept and embrace Asperger Syndrome. It has brought me some very real healing.

Life is too short for us to be anything other than true to who we are. People who have Asperger Syndrome (and who, unlike me, do not deny that part of themselves) do us a great service – not just because of any particular contributions that they might make to the world, but because they are essentially true to themselves in a way that typical people tend not to be.

This can make life very difficult and uncomfortable for them as well as for the people around them, but Asperger Syndrome has a lot to offer the world. Even if you set aside the issue of formal diagnosis, the characteristic traits of AS have been responsible for some of the world's greatest achievements right throughout history.

Aspies can be difficult; they can challenge; and they can take us right out of our comfort zones. But if we are equal to the challenge, we have a great deal to gain and a great deal to learn from Asperger Syndrome.

ASPERGER SYNDROME – UNLOCKING THE MYSTERY

Chapter 1

BUMPING INTO LAMP POSTS AND STEPPING ON TOES

REASONS AND REACTIONS

Just imagine that you look out your window tomorrow morning, and you see someone you don't know walking into a lamp post. What would your attitude be? You could be pretty sure of one thing – he didn't do it on purpose. He might, for example:

- have some problems with his eyesight

- have had too much to drink

- have been distracted (perhaps he had a problem on his mind; perhaps he was just thinking about something else; perhaps something else diverted his attention).

And how do you think you would react? Would you laugh; would you be sympathetic and offer help; or would you turn away?

I suppose the answer would depend on your personality. But it would also depend on whatever impression you had formed of (1) the person who had walked into the lamp post and (2) the cause of the accident.

- **The person**: I imagine you would be more sympathetic if the person seemed vulnerable and in need of help. If he or she was a young child, seemed to be alone, was clearly hurt, and started to cry, you would probably think it was heartless to do anything except try to help. The same would be true if the person seemed old and infirm.

■ **The cause**: Of the three possible reasons listed above (eyesight, distraction and alcohol) you would probably be most sympathetic and understanding if you believed that the person had some kind of visual impairment.

So what have lamp posts got to do with Asperger Syndrome?

Sometimes it seems as if people with AS go through life 'bumping into lamp posts'. They do this generally by breaking social rules and expectations. And just as with lamp posts, how other people react depends mostly on how much they understand both the Aspie and the reason. *That makes it very important for us to do all we can to understand Asperger Syndrome.*

This book is about attitudes, and so before I wrote it, I did some informal research on attitudes. What I found out just confirmed what I had heard people say for years and what I believed myself – among people who are actually involved in the world of AS (Aspies, family, carers etc.), there seem to be some commonly held opinions. Examples of these are: (1) in general attitudes to AS are unduly harsh, judgemental and negative; (2) people need to 'be more positive about Asperger Syndrome'; (3) if attitudes were more positive this would be of benefit not only to individual Aspies but also to the world in general, because AS has a lot to contribute to the world; and (4) in order to be more positive, the primary thing that is needed is to increase the level of understanding.

The idea of increasing understanding makes sense on many levels, for to understand is to forgive after all, and a forgiving attitude is the opposite of a judgemental one. So we will need to do some exploring to try and get beneath the surface of AS and reach a deeper understanding.

Let's start by looking at a few basic questions. Why do people with AS go through life 'bumping into lamp posts' by breaking social rules? Why do they do things that cause offence and make life more difficult?

MIND BLINDNESS

When you understand AS as a form of 'mind blindness', things start to make sense. But what does the term 'mind blindness' mean? Obviously it does not mean you are physically blind, but at its most basic level, it means what it sounds like it means – it is a deficit in being able to see (or assess with any degree of accuracy) what is going on in the mind of another person.

NON-VERBAL COMMUNICATION

Let's think radically about this – how do any of us know what is going on in each other's mind? There are two main ways – by means of verbal communication and by means of non-verbal communication. Verbal communication often really just means written communication (like this book for example!) but when there is some person-to-person element, such as when two people meet or even talk on the phone, there is always some element of non-verbal communication – facial expression, tone of voice and so on. (To take a simple example, if I am giving a talk, and I notice someone's eyes glazing over and he or she begins to yawn, that can communicate to me non-verbally that that person is bored.) Non-verbal communication also includes a huge number of unwritten assumptions about how things are 'supposed' to operate between people.

In general Aspies have little problem with verbal communication. In fact they are often highly skilled or even gifted at it. That is why they are often excellent at on-line communication and using instant messenger programmes and so on. But for whatever reason, non-verbal communication can be like a big black hole to them – a lamp post that they cannot see, so to speak! And when you really take this on board, it can be a key to understanding what lies at the root of AS difficulties.

Yet non-verbal communication is a vital aspect of communication. Animals need to be very good at it in order to survive. They cannot use verbal communication the way humans do, yet without words they manage to communicate important things like anger, warning, greeting, welcome – without words they are able to run families and communities, discipline their young and even to love.

Non-verbal communication is a far bigger and more important part of communication than we realise. It helps us, for example, to:

- read facial expressions

- hear the real meaning and intention in what other people say

- understand unwritten rules

- understand what is expected of us.

Just think what it would be like if you were unable to see lamp posts – if you were 'lamp post blind' so to speak. If you bumped into one you would know all about it. You might even remember where it was so you could avoid it the next time – but you still mightn't be able to see it.

It is possible for Aspies to learn non-verbal communication and to improve over time. But we need to appreciate that it may always be a bit like a foreign language for them, and it will not come easy. So even if they do learn it, it may never feel completely natural, or as if it is their mother tongue, so to speak.

STEPPING ON TOES

When we compare an Aspie breaking a social rule to a visually impaired man walking into a lamp post, it is easy to be positive and understanding. But we need to extend the analogy a bit. Let's think of it like this. In theory you might be tolerant and understanding of someone who was visually impaired if he walked into a lamp post, because that does not hurt *you* in any way. But how would you feel about someone who kept standing on your toe day after day?

Both these analogies are helpful for understanding AS, because sometimes AS people do hurt themselves by 'walking into lamp posts', and sometimes they hurt other people by 'stepping on their toes' so to speak.

How would you react if you were walking down the street and someone who appeared perfectly 'normal' stepped – apparently care-lessly – on your toe? You might think he was stupid; or you might think he was doing it on purpose; you might be angry with him; or you might make a note to avoid him the next time. And these are all things that happen when AS people break social rules.

When you think of it like this, it is easy to understand why over time a lot of Aspies end up being harshly judged and misunderstood, feeling they are stupid, and becoming isolated. Obviously, this kind of hostility or judgement is bad news for individual Aspies, but assuming that there is a link between AS and giftedness, it may also mean that people who are gifted and who would otherwise have a lot to give to the world, are being marginalised and their talents wasted.

Here is where understanding can really help. For as soon as you realised that the person who 'stood on your toe' was visually impaired, your reaction would probably be very different. You would be less likely to judge him, and it would be easier to accept that he didn't mean to 'cause offence'. You would probably want to help him. You might see, for example, that it could be very useful to explain to him where obstacles lay, so he could avoid them in the future.

> An Aspie goes through life breaking the social rules rather in the way that someone with a visual impairment might bump into lamp posts and step on people's toes.

A SNAPSHOT

There are various ways of understanding Asperger Syndrome and it can be helpful to look at things from different angles, but it is important to remember that we cannot be too black and white about any of them. It is not true, for example, to say that people with AS 'cannot read non-verbal communication'. The truth is more subtle than that. It is probably more accurate to say that NT's are generally much *better* at non-verbal communication than Aspies.

But even among NT's there is a lot of variation. Some people are more skilful than others at non-verbal communication. It is generally agreed, for example, that females are naturally more skilful than males. It can therefore sometimes be helpful to think of Aspies as being extremely male!

Sometimes Aspies can cause offence in very subtle ways, and we need to recognise that these may be due to AS mind blindness as well, for subtle difficulties can have a big impact over time in creating a negative impression. Let me give you an example of something that happened one day while I was writing this book. It was just a trivial incident, but as a snapshot of a moment in time, it can give a bit of a flavour of Asperger Syndrome at its most subtle.

I was sitting at my laptop trying to get some work done, when all of a sudden my 18-year-old son, Kenneth, walked past.

'What are you writing a book about anyway?' he asked.

I was a bit stuck at the time, so I quite liked the idea of stopping for a chat with him. Because Kenneth has Asperger Syndrome I thought he might be able to give me an interesting angle. So I started onto a lengthy explanation.

But I should have known better. A chat wasn't what he was looking for. And within seconds I could see I was rambling on too much for his liking, and he interrupted me.

'Just tell me in a sentence,' he said. To me he sounded snappy and irritated.

'Why do you want me to tell you in a sentence?' I asked.

He pondered that for a few moments before giving any reply, and when I heard his reason I laughed. It was so honest and so typical of him.

'It might save me the bother of reading the book!' he said.

LOOKING MORE CLOSELY

A subtle abrasiveness

As I said, it was only a little incident, but it was a very typical one, and it offers us some insights into AS. What are they?

There are a few things. For a start, there was a sort of abrasive feel to the whole transaction, and that alone is very typical of Aspergers. It was a subtle feeling, but it was still off-putting. It was hard to put your finger on exactly why it felt abrasive. Even though I laughed, it felt somehow too blunt and abrupt.

That abrasive feeling can be hard to pin down, so you can imagine how hard it can be for an Aspie to be aware of it or to understand it. But people find it uncomfortable to be around. They may not know quite what it is they are uncomfortable with or why; they just know they want to avoid it. This is a subtle kind of phenomenon, but it needs to be acknowledged, because over time it can be at least part of the reason why Aspies end up alone and isolated.

By the way, I can't actually remember if I managed to do what he asked that day and 'tell him in a sentence'. But if I did, the sentence would have been a very simple one. As simple as this maybe:

People need to be more positive about Asperger Syndrome.

We didn't discuss it any further that day but I have been able to ascertain his views on the subject in the meantime, and they are pretty similar to the views of most other people: that (1) people need to be more positive about AS and (2) they would be more positive if they understood it.

Identifying blind spots in the snapshot

Let's take a closer look at the snapshot and analyse where the blind spots lay. Each of us, naturally enough, had our own point of view or perspective.

What was mine that day?

My writing was important to me, and I didn't like it when Kenneth was so dismissive about it. Even though I knew he meant no harm, I still felt a bit put down by his bluntness. He seemed rude and abrupt.

And what was Kenneth's perspective?

He was just being honest and direct, and his point of view was a simple one – he wanted information, not conversation. And he is definitely a man who doesn't like to waste words!

My perspective was not even on his radar screen, so to speak. It never entered his head that I might have liked him to show more of an interest or appreciation of what I was doing. That meant he had no idea that he came across as rude or abrupt. And that is a common phenomenon with Asperger Syndrome.

People with AS have certain blind spots. Once we know and accept this:

- NT's should be less inclined to take it personally or be offended when Aspies 'step on their toes'

- Aspies should feel less stupid when they do

- NT's should be in a better position to understand AS

- it should be easier to identify and communicate where 'blind spots' lie.

AS and extremes

But there is another way to look at the little snapshot I described. Kenneth is a teenager, and a lot of teenage boys are curt and abrupt like that. From that point of view, you could see it as a typical teen encounter. So was he behaving like a typical Aspie or was he behaving like a typical teenager? The answer is both really. And the fact that the little incident can validly be seen in both ways gives us another insight into Asperger Syndrome. Here's how.

AS is a complex and mysterious condition, and people can spend years trying to get to grips with it. I know I have, but one of the most helpful things I have ever heard anyone say was simply this:

People with AS are just like everyone else, only more so.

In other words, if you are dealing with AS, you can expect things to be extreme. If you do, you won't be far wrong! So when Kenneth gave me the answer he did, he was behaving like a teenager. And yes, he is a typical teen – *only more so*. That is a crucial point.

The difference between AS and 'normality' is often just one of degree. Moderation does not come easily to the person with Asperger Syndrome. It is actually hard to find anything in Asperger Syndrome that is not in all of us. And that is really good news because, at least in theory, it should make AS easier to understand.

Chapter 2

SEEING STARS

A MATTER OF CHOICE

When someone is in a difficult situation and manages to stay positive and rise above it, there is always something very admirable about it. Once long ago I came across a verse that conjures up the feeling of what I mean. It went like this:

> *Two men looked out the same prison bars;*
> *One sees mud and the other stars.*
>
> Frederick Langbridge

I can't remember where I heard those words, but I think there is something very inspiring about them. Why? Because they speak of an eternal truth; one that every one of us can identify with. And it is simply this: there are always two ways of looking at things. And no matter what we come up against in life, how we see it is at the end of the day up to us.

There are other analogies about this too of course – like when we talk about how 'you need to look at both sides of the coin' or that 'there are two sides to every story' or 'you can see the glass as half full or half empty'.

The important thing is this: whether we choose to look on the positive or the negative side of things, both are valid and true. They are just different ways of seeing the same thing. It is just as true to say the glass is half-full as to say it is half-empty. It just depends on how you look at it.

As for the two men who looked out from the prison that starry night, they both had the same view, yet what they saw was completely different. What they saw were just different aspects of the same reality. For on a clear night both mud and stars are there to be seen.

And when it comes to Asperger Syndrome, the same thing applies. There are two sides to the AS story as well. There is mud and there are stars. Both ways of seeing things are valid and true. They are just different aspects of the one reality.

On a clear night both mud and stars are there to be seen.

A BRIEF LOOK AT THE NEGATIVE SIDE

Being positive means looking at the stars rather than at the mud, so to speak. But it doesn't mean we should pretend there is no mud. We need to acknowledge that mud exists even if we don't want to focus on it. So before we go on, let's take a very quick look at the 'mud'.

If you are dealing with AS in your life you don't need me to tell you this, but the everyday reality of living with AS can be very difficult. Here are a few of the reasons:

- Some Aspies have behaviour problems that make them very hard to rear. It is hard to describe the severity of these problems to anyone who has not had to deal with them, but they can be far harder to manage than any kind of 'normal' behaviour problems. This can put enormous strain on families.

- Social difficulties are an inevitable part of the condition, and this can make life very hard. Aspies often end up alone, lonely and isolated.

- Some Aspies can be extremely hard for teachers to educate and manage in the classroom.

- Even though they are often very intelligent and even gifted, they are likely to under-achieve both at school and in the workplace.

- Although it is hard to know how much of this is a part of the condition and how much is the result of living with it in an unforgiving world, many Aspies suffer from secondary difficulties such as mental health issues, anxiety and depression.

- Overall Asperger Syndrome is a complex and 'hidden' disability which makes it hard to understand and easy to judge.

I should point out here that this is not supposed to be a comprehensive list. It is just meant to give a flavour of some of the difficulties associated with AS – and they are very real difficulties. Even though this book is about the positive side of Asperger Syndrome, there is no point in brushing the difficulties under the carpet.

A BRIEF LOOK AT THE POSITIVE SIDE

But there is a lot about AS that is positive as well. So let's take a very quick look at the positive side now:

- ✓ Aspies are generally very honest. The direct, blunt manner that we associate with AS can seem tactless and can be very challenging at times, but there is a refreshing honesty about it as well.

- ✓ Aspies have brains that work differently from most people's brains, and the world needs the Aspergers brain.

- ✓ Typically they are very strong-minded people and have the kind of determination that can help them achieve great things and overcome great odds.

✓ They can be very intelligent and even gifted.

✓ The traits and characteristics of AS can be very useful, and have made important contributions to progress and advancement throughout history.

✓ Aspies tend to be unusual and interesting people. Often they are a bit eccentric, and eccentric people add to the richness of life!

✓ They have an unusual take on life that can be refreshing and challenging, and in the right circumstances typical Aspie behaviour can seem very funny.

Again this is not meant to be a comprehensive list of all that is positive about Asperger Syndrome. It is just meant as a brief overview of some of the things you could decide to focus on if you were looking at AS from a positive angle – if you were to look at the stars instead of the mud, that is.

A balanced view?

If we focus on the positive side of AS will that give us a one-sided view? Maybe so. But on the other hand maybe that's what we need sometimes, for it is far more common for people to do the opposite and focus on the negatives. And maybe that is inevitable, because so many of the Aspies who come to attention are the ones who have problems and need help.

But if attitudes were more positive, there would be some real advantages. For example: (1) it would help Aspies feel better about themselves; (2) people who suspect they might have AS would be more likely to come forward for assessment.

Easier said than done

Is it possible for us to look out and 'see stars' just as the prisoner in the verse did? Yes, it is possible. But is it easy? Far from it, in many cases.

When you are living with the problems every day, being positive and understanding is much easier said than done. I have seen this in other people. But I also know it from my own personal experience, and that's probably more meaningful. So let me tell you a bit more of my own story.

PART 1 – ASPERGER MUM

First we need to go back in time ten years or so. At that time I had two children – a daughter of about 17 and a son of about eight. My daughter had been very easy and straightforward to raise. I am not saying she was perfect. There were all the normal ups and downs that you would expect with a teenage daughter, but overall there had been no major problems. She and I got on well and she was a normal, healthy, friendly, easy-going and good-natured child. Even when she was young, I hadn't had many problems with her behaviour.

Then my son, Kenneth, came along and the story was the complete opposite. From the very start there was something about him that seemed different. It is almost impossible to sum up exactly what this was, though.

I could sense even when he was a baby that there was something about him that seemed very sensitive and vulnerable. There then followed years of heartache and problems – what kind of heartache was it? It was the kind of heartache only someone who has been there can understand. It is the heartache of a mother who knows that the son she loves is unhappy and no matter what she does, or how hard she tries, nothing seems to work. There is nothing she can do to make him happy or to fix things, and she has no idea what to do next or where to turn.

And what kind of problems? The list is endless – problems with behaviour, with eating, with sleeping. Bizarre problems that no one seemed to understand. Why did he not want to join in with other children, for example? Why did he get upset and cause a scene over weird things like which door of the car he got out of? Why did he refuse to do a thing he was told? Why was he not doing any work at school? Or playing with the other children? I tried every avenue I could think of to find some kind of solution, but the problems seemed insoluble and they just wouldn't go away.

Even though I went through a complex mixture of emotions when he was diagnosed, one of the first things I felt was relief. Why? In retrospect I think it is because it took away some of my guilt. Let me explain what I mean by that.

By the time Kenneth was diagnosed, I felt pretty much like a failure as a Mum. I had spent about nine years doing everything I could humanly think of to get him 'sorted out', but it seemed that my best efforts were to no avail. I had a sinking feeling in my heart because there was something about him that made him so different and so difficult, that I feared he would never find his place in the world, and nobody on earth would ever find a way of 'managing' him – no school, no teacher and certainly not me!

Then when I found out he 'had Asperger Syndrome' I could let myself off the hook a bit, so to speak, and for a while I was able to feel a little less guilty. I began to see how all the difficulties of the last nine years mightn't be my fault after all. And they mightn't be his fault either – they mightn't be anyone's fault, come to think about it!

That feeling of relief is a common one when a child has been diagnosed with AS. I have discovered that from talking to other parents in the same position in the intervening years. It is a relief not only from guilt but also from confusion, at least to some extent. Diagnosis after years of searching, frustration and bewilderment can seem like a kind of answer, and to offer some hope of help and direction.

PART 2 – ASPERGER WRITER

Kenneth's diagnosis was a big turning point in both our lives. I reacted in the same way that a lot of parents do in the same position. Right away I launched myself into finding out all I could about AS. I dread to think now how many man-hours I must have spent on the computer, reading books, going to talks and courses about Asperger Syndrome, and talking to professionals about my son.

By the time he got his diagnosis, I was finding it next to impossible to manage his behaviour, but then I began an ABA (applied behaviour analysis) programme with him, and it was a great help. There were still an awful lot of problems, but some things improved. I became very interested in different approaches to behaviour management, and I began to think up and try out different ideas and gather up any tips and strategies that I came across. Before long I was doing this intensively, to the point where it became like some strange kind of all-absorbing hobby for me!

I got ideas from anywhere I could find them, and began to record them on the computer. Then I began to catalogue them into some kind of order, and eventually I approached Jessica Kingsley with the idea that these might usefully be made into a book. By that time I had put so much energy into the whole project that it seemed crazy to think it should all be for one child. I could see no point in other parents having to re-invent the wheel. The result of all this was my book *Parenting a Child with Asperger Syndrome: 200 Tips and Strategies*.

That book was a very practical book, and it reflected where I was at that time, for when you are dealing with a child with AS, it is very useful to have a range of tips and strategies to try. It was certainly an interesting time for me, for you have to be inventive when you are the parent of an Aspie child. They say that if you can learn to manage a child with Asperger Syndrome, it will help you manage any child – and I can see why!

I definitely learnt a lot during those years, but the most important thing that I came to realise was this: in order to be truly loving to my son, I needed to accept him exactly as he was. And I could see very clearly that his AS was very much part of him, and a part that was never going to go away. So I needed to accept and be positive about his AS as well.

> *If you can learn to manage a child with Asperger Syndrome, that will help you manage any child.*

PART 3 – ASPERGER PROFESSIONAL

You might think that after all this, I would have had enough of Asperger Syndrome, but I can't have! About five years ago the NAS (National Autistic Society) was established in Northern Ireland and I ended up working for them. It was one of those things that just seemed to be meant to be at the time. I'll tell you how it came about.

One of the aspects of AS that had always saddened me most was the fact that Aspies find it so hard either to make or to keep friends, and that they can end up very lonely. I had seen this in my son, and I talked to other AS Mums as well, so I knew it was a common problem. Surely there must be a solution, I thought. Perhaps there was a way in which children like Kenneth could have befrienders?

Then, around the time when I was thinking of this, I happened to see an advert in the local paper saying that the NAS were looking for someone to set up a Befriending Service in Northern Ireland. I didn't even know the NAS had such a thing as a Befriending Service, but I knew right away that this was the job for me, and I applied and got it.

I learned a lot from running the Befriending Service. It gave me the chance to get some professional training in ASD, to meet a lot of professionals and experts in the ASD world, and also to meet and visit the homes of many people whose lives are affected by ASD.

There was something I had begun to notice over the years. People had widely different attitudes to AS, depending on what they knew about it:

- If they had heard something from the media, they often saw it as a fascinating condition.

- If they knew little but had come up against the 'wrong side' of it, they tended to be judgemental and dismissive.

But often the people at the coal face, so to speak – Aspies and their families in particular – had an attitude that was genuinely inspiring. These were the people with the real difficulties to deal with on a day-to-day basis, and they often felt exhausted and under-appreciated. But above and beyond that, I saw a great deal of courage and warmth. And I also saw attitudes towards Asperger Syndrome which were genuinely appreciative. Naturally they had days when they saw nothing but mud, but when it mattered, they were also able to see the stars.

It seems to work something like this. When people have to work hard to understand AS, either in themselves or in someone close to them, it is very likely that they will automatically become more appreciative and positive. And that can make a great difference to the success and happiness of the individual Aspie. By success, by the way, I don't necessarily mean success in the world's terms (such as exam results or well-paid jobs, though this may be true as well).

Here's what I mean. Every one of us has a basic need to feel we are OK and accepted for who we really are. When someone has AS, then that AS is an intrinsic part of who he really is: if attitudes to AS are negative and judgemental, this can be hard on individual Aspies. But the good news is this: if a person with Asperger Syndrome has even a few people in his life who are positive, understanding and supportive, then even if the rest of the world seems hostile, at some deep level he is much more likely to be happy about who he really is.

PART 4 – PERSONAL CRISIS

How I went about things might sound a bit intense. And if you know about how intensity and Asperger Syndrome often go hand in hand, and if you know how AS tends to run in families, then you're probably not surprised that I ended up getting a diagnosis myself about two years ago.

The significant thing is this. Ever since Kenneth was diagnosed, I had suspected that I had AS myself. He and I used to joke about it from time to time. But it took me till two years ago to finally go for an assessment. Why was I slow to investigate it? I suppose the only way to answer is to say that I was in denial. I was perfectly well aware that there was a genetic link to AS, and I could see all the traits in myself, but I did not want to know.

And I have to confess that in the end I did not even go that willingly for the diagnosis. There was a long saga of difficulties and traumas, and I eventually got to the point where it almost seemed like I didn't have a choice. I had to have a bit of a breakdown before I finally admitted the truth. Part of the truth was that I had AS myself. Another part was that my attitude was not as positive as I thought. I could see the positive side of things in theory. I could be positive as an AS Mum, AS writer, AS professional, but it was another thing to be an actual Aspie.

Before my diagnosis, I was cutting off the AS part of myself. I never set out to do that, of course. Nevertheless it was what happened. But there is something that I didn't find out until recently and it is this: when you cut off some part of yourself, you can end up paying a high price, for you may be cutting off more than you realise.

For whatever reason, somewhere along the way, I had closed a door to the Asperger part of myself. But in doing so I also closed a door to some of the happiness, creativity, fulfilment and freedom that we can only ever find when we are true to ourselves.

I wonder how many other people the same thing could apply to.

A COMPLEX CONDITION

Obviously trying to understand AS is very worthwhile, for the more deeply we understand it, the more positive we can be. But it is a huge undertaking, for it is a highly complex condition. It is hard to answer even the most basic question 'What is Asperger Syndrome?' in a meaningful and succinct way. And yet we need to find an answer, for we have no hope of appreciating something if we don't even understand what it is.

Maybe before we delve any deeper we should first look at Asperger Syndrome from the outside, and come up with a description of what it looks like. That should be a straightforward matter at least.

Or so you might think… But if you did you would be wrong!

Chapter 3

THE BIG UMBRELLA

PICTURES OF ASPERGER SYNDROME

It is well known that Asperger Syndrome is a complicated and hard condition to understand or explain, but more than that, it is hard even to explain what it looks like. In fact if you were to ask 20 different outsiders the question 'What does AS look like?', there's a good chance you would get 20 answers, and they would all be different, at least to some extent. Let's have a look at how this could possibly be.

I want you to try a little exercise.

Think for a moment about Asperger Syndrome... What kind of picture comes into your head?

Now read through the checklist on the next page. It contains an alphabetical list of words or descriptions. You are being asked which of them you would think of as being associated with AS in some way. Try not to think about the questions too carefully. Just give the first answers that come to your head.

The checklist however is not meant as a comprehensive description of Asperger Syndrome, but it does give us some idea of how wide-ranging the condition can be. If you want to know what AS 'looks like' there are three keywords to keep in mind. These words are 'extremes', 'variety' and 'range'.

PICTURES OF AS – A CHECKLIST

	Associated with AS	Not associated with AS
Arrogant?	☐	☐
Artistic?	☐	☐
Autistic?	☐	☐
Avoids people?	☐	☐
Badly behaved?	☐	☐
Computer nerd?	☐	☐
Creative?	☐	☐
Demanding?	☐	☐
Dependent?	☐	☐
Depressed?	☐	☐
Different?	☐	☐
Feels he is much more intelligent than others?	☐	☐
Feels he is much more stupid than others?	☐	☐
Finds specific subjects such as maths very difficult?	☐	☐
Finds specific subjects such as maths very easy?	☐	☐
Frustrating?	☐	☐
Genius?	☐	☐
Gifted?	☐	☐
Gullible?	☐	☐
Humour is highly developed?	☐	☐
Humour is poor or absent?	☐	☐
Insensitive?	☐	☐
Intelligent?	☐	☐
In your face?	☐	☐
Isolated?	☐	☐

	Associated with AS	Not associated with AS
Lacking in common sense?	☐	☐
Lacking in confidence?	☐	☐
Lonely?	☐	☐
Misfit?	☐	☐
Naïve?	☐	☐
Nervous?	☐	☐
Over-confident?	☐	☐
Over-friendly (i.e. inappropriately so)?	☐	☐
Over-sensitive?	☐	☐
Rude?	☐	☐
Self-effacing?	☐	☐
Self-obsessed?	☐	☐
Sensitive?	☐	☐
Shy?	☐	☐
Special needs?	☐	☐
Talented?	☐	☐
Talks too little?	☐	☐
Talks too much?	☐	☐
Tortuous?	☐	☐
Tortured?	☐	☐
Unusual?	☐	☐

A WIDE SPECTRUM

Quite a selection isn't it? But I have seen every single one of the descriptions on that list in various people with Asperger Syndrome, and attributed to the fact that they have Asperger Syndrome. In other words any of those things could potentially be regarded as 'symptoms' of AS.

Extremes

You will have noticed how some of the descriptions directly contradict each other (e.g. sensitive and insensitive; or talks too little and talks too much). That is because AS is a condition of extremes. When you bear that in mind, it can be a great help to understanding its various traits and aspects.

To get an idea of what the experience of AS is like, sometimes all you need to do is to think of a time when you experienced the same thing and then imagine a much more intense version of a particular aspect of the same experience and feelings. Multiply it by a factor of, say, ten. So it works two ways. Understanding ourselves better helps us understand AS, and understanding AS better helps us understand ourselves. And who knows what we may discover along the way – for often the AS parts of ourselves are the most interesting parts of all!

People with AS can be extremely different to each other; but as well as that sometimes one person with AS can manifest completely opposite extremes at different times. For example the same person can sometimes come across as extremely arrogant at one time and extremely self-effacing at another time, depending on the circumstances. Or a child with AS might be extremely well-behaved at school and extremely badly-behaved at home. Or maybe the other way round.

One of the problems about AS being a condition of extremes is that it makes the whole condition much less clear cut. If 'symptoms' of AS seem like an extreme version of 'normal' difficulties that means:

- it is easier for people to go undiagnosed

- it is easier for diagnosis not to be taken seriously. When that happens, people may either make little of it or deny it.

I remember when my son was small, just like every other Asperger's Mum, I used to worry about him an awful lot. But at the start I had no idea that he had Asperger Syndrome. In fact I had never even heard of it. When I had problems managing his behaviour, I really thought it must be my fault, and I felt completely inadequate as a Mum. Sometimes I tried to confide in other people about the problems I was having with him, but it was very hard to put across the severity. None of the problems seemed that different from 'normal' problems. For example, if I said I could not get him to eat, or sleep, or conform, or whatever, they would compare my situation to theirs, and they would say something like 'Don't worry, I have problems getting my son to eat too.'

People say things like that because they are trying to be reassuring, but it can actually have the opposite effect, because in my mind if my son's difficulties were just 'normal' ones, then I felt I should be dealing with them better, so I was even more convinced that I was the one with the problem. But I could see that he was not 'growing out of it' the way I hoped he would, and that the problems were much more extreme than 'normal'.

> Understanding ourselves better helps us understand AS, and understanding AS better helps us understand ourselves.

Variety and range

Another thing we can learn from the above checklist (Pictures of AS) is that it gives us a clearer idea of how wide-ranging the condition is. There have been various lists compiled recently of some of the traits which are commonly found in AS. One in particular extends to over 100 traits! In fact, it is because AS covers such a wide spectrum of people that it is referred to as a 'spectrum disorder'.

It is important to grasp this first and most basic thing about Asperger Syndrome. It is like a very big umbrella which covers a wide range of people who may manifest it in very different ways, and to varying degrees. I saw exactly this expressed on the NAS website recently, although it used more official language.

> *For all those in the autism continuum there is one out-standing feature and that is the variability of effects on individuals. This is far more than is associated with any other condition.*
>
> *Lones 1996*

If you could look at a random selection of different people who had all been given the label 'Asperger' how would you tell them apart from a random selection of people who did not have Aspergers? You might have a vague impression that there was something about the Aspies that they had in common with each other. But you would probably find it hard to tie down exactly what that something was. And if you were to make out your own list of adjectives that describe the different Aspies, you might be surprised at how much variety it contained. That is why one of the key words in answering this question 'What does AS look like?' has to be the word 'variety'.

Another key word has to be 'range', and this is because there is such a wide range of people who come under what is known as the Asperger umbrella. AS is wide-ranging in many ways. For example it can cover people with a wide range of ability and intelligence levels.

THE PROBLEM WITH STEREOTYPES

Whatever way you view labels, there is no way of getting round the fact that a diagnosis of AS is a kind of label. One of the downsides of labels is that they tend to turn into stereotypes.

There are always problems with stereotypes because by their very nature they tie things down too narrowly. People can easily get a fixed idea in their heads about what AS looks like, and not realise that their picture is far too narrow. It is worse than meaningless to make AS into a stereotype because it covers a wide range in the first place. Nevertheless it happens a lot.

If you have one specific picture of AS in your head, and then you come across someone who looks completely different from that picture, you may find it hard to believe that that other person also has AS. In fact often you may not want to believe it. Let's look at a few examples of how this might happen and the kind of problem it can cause.

Example 1 – a guilty Mum

First let's imagine you are the Mum of an AS child who is very badly behaved and you meet a Mum of a very well-behaved AS child. You might not like to believe that the other child has the same condition as your child. Why not? Because you are a typical Mum, and like all Mums you go through phases when you feel guilty about your child's problems, and you blame yourself because you have so little control over his behaviour. When you found out he had AS, it took away a little bit of the guilt. So when you come across a well-behaved AS child, you would rather not believe he really has AS too, because it brings up your feelings of guilt once again.

In your mind maybe the other Mum has been a success where you have been a failure, and you think you ought to have been able to sort out your child's behaviour problems by now – maybe if one AS Mum can get her child to behave well then any AS Mum should be able to do the same. That however is simply not true.

The point here is this. A lot of AS children have extreme behaviour problems and they can be so hard to manage that you could say they are 'in a league of their own'. Someone who has never had to deal with this will probably never be able to really understand it. But not all AS children are the same. Most display at least strange and eccentric behaviour, but they are not all extremely hard to manage, and even the ones who are 'difficult' can be easier or harder in certain situations or with certain people.

Example 2 – famous musician

Now let's take a different example. Let's imagine you are a successful, world-famous personality in some field or other. It could be some form of academics. Or drama. Or IT maybe. Or perhaps you are an artist. It could be any number of things. But for the sake of the illustration let's take it that you are a musician. You do actually 'have AS' in the sense that if you were to get an assessment you would amply fit the criteria, but you have never been diagnosed. Maybe you have never even considered it as a possibility.

You may have had social difficulties all your life, but you have masked them well and kept them to yourself to a large degree. Sometimes these problems get on top of you, but you are so used to them that you take them to be normal, and just see them as part of who you are. Looking back on your life you realise that you have under-performed in certain areas – at school for example. But on the other hand you have over-performed in the world of music, which is your passion and probably even your obsession. You have had real difficulties managing certain areas of your life – especially when it comes to relating to other people. You have probably suffered from bouts of depression, but you have got around your difficulties – maybe at times by using alcohol or drugs, but mostly by immersing yourself in the music world.

How would you feel if someone suggested that you might have Asperger Syndrome? I don't think you would be at the top of the queue looking for a diagnosis. Why not? Perhaps it has just never occurred to you. But if you have, you are bound to have a certain fixed notion about what AS is, what the label means, and what it looks like, and you are not particularly keen on the idea of applying that label to yourself.

You may not know much about AS, but maybe you have heard that it is a form of autism. That can be enough to put some people off. Even the word 'autism' carries negative connotations in many people's eyes. For some people the word 'autism' can conjure up a picture of someone disabled and maybe a bit weird. If that was your image of autism or Asperger Syndrome, would you want to look into the idea that you have AS yourself? I don't think so.

Both of these examples show that it is easy to get a picture in your head about what AS is and what it looks like which is far too narrow. And they also show some of the problems that this can cause. The first example highlighted the basic problem of guilt and inappropriate responsibility; and the second highlighted the problem of under-diagnosis.

Some other problems with stereotypes

Stereotyping always tends to be misleading, but this is probably even more true in the case of AS because it is such a wide-ranging condition. It is thus very easy for a vicious cycle to develop in the following way:

- There is probably a lot of under-diagnosis of people who may have real (but perhaps subtle) problems, but who do not fit the stereotype.

- Diagnosis of people with extreme problems and difficulties is more common.

- This creates an unrepresentative impression of AS, i.e. those who are at the more able/less extreme end are under-represented. Or, to put it more crassly, AS gets a 'bad name'.

- The stereotype is strengthened. This reinforces the first point, and so the cycle strengthens.

AS SUBGROUPS

Another interesting consequence of AS being such a big umbrella is that it is possible to loosely identify certain Aspie 'subgroups'. I am not saying that these are official subgroups, but I have heard all the subgroups listed below talked about informally (for example by parents or at professional meetings) so presumably they are worth looking at. At the very least, they can offer some insight into how people perceive the categories of people who come under the 'big umbrella'.

Aspies are sometimes divided into, for example:

- **The 'Gifted' and the 'Special Needs' Subgroups**: Aspies often have a jagged profile of abilities and there may be specific areas which they find very difficult. Because of that and also because of social and behavioural issues, they may be classed as having 'special needs'. However, people with AS are generally of at least normal intelligence, and some are recognised to be gifted. The more we can dispel the myths and stereotypes surrounding Asperger Syndrome, the more likely it seems that gifted people will come forward for diagnosis.

- **The 'Pleasant' and the 'Unpleasant' Subgroups**: 'Pleasant' Aspies are extremely diligent, keen to get things right and please others, whereas 'Unpleasant' Aspies are a law unto themselves and seem to care about pleasing no one. 'Unpleasant' Aspies are more likely to come to attention and receive diagnosis and support.

- **The 'Creative' and the 'Scientific' Subgroups**: 'Creative' Aspies will be very interested in things like music and art, whereas 'Scientific' Aspies will be very interested in things like maths and computers. Both Creative and Scientific Aspies can be very talented, determined, focused and even obsessive in their own areas.

- **The 'High Achiever' and the 'Under-performer' Subgroups**: Some Aspies go on to achieve great and remarkable things and may even receive world acclaim. Unfortunately it is much more common for the opposite to happen, and Aspies often end up in jobs for which they are completely over-qualified (at least in terms of ability), or even in no job at all. It is worth pointing out though that sometimes things can change, and an Underr-performer can go on to become a High Achiever in later years.

- **The 'Obvious' and the 'Subtle' Subgroups**: The difficulties of people with AS can range from very obvious to very subtle. Some Aspies are very hard to 'spot' unless either you are an expert or you are very experienced and insightful. For example, as children, some have major behaviour problems. They can be extremely demanding, hard to manage, and drive the people around them to distraction. They don't fit in, and they don't seem to care who they upset. There is no way that children like this are going to go unnoticed.

  Then at the opposite extreme, there are Aspies who go to extreme pains to fit in and be pleasing. These people may have strange, eccentric behaviour but their difficulties can be very subtle. These are the people who are more likely to suffer in silence and go without diagnosis, either for a long time or forever.

SO WHAT NEXT?

It might be very interesting to look at the vast range of people who come under the AS umbrella, but if we are trying to understand and appreciate AS it doesn't take us much further. In fact it can leave us even more confused – for how on earth can all these different descriptions and sub-groups belong to the same condition?

Obviously AS is a mysterious and confusing condition. People call it a 'spectrum disorder', but really that is just another way of saying that it is like a big umbrella. It is useful to have it described in that way of course, but a description is just a description. It is not an explanation. Now we are going to have to try to get beneath the surface and understand it!

> Given the right opportunity, environment and encouragement, an AS under-performer can go on to achieve success in later years.

Chapter 4

WRONG PLANET
SYNDROME

A COMMON BOND

In the last chapter we saw that Asperger Syndrome is like a big umbrella covering a wide range of people who can, at least to outward appearances, be extremely different to each other. But behind the appearances, they must all have something in common. What is it? If we could find out, we would be one step nearer to understanding Asperger Syndrome.

One very obvious way of finding out is simply to listen to Aspies. Is there anything in particular that they all seem to say about themselves? Yes, there is. All Aspies seem, in one way or another, to say they feel like outsiders and in some way different and apart from other people.

They may use different analogies to express this. For example they may say they feel like a visitor to a foreign country who doesn't understand the local language and customs – or like they are on the 'wrong planet'. But whatever language they use, it boils down to the same thing. The common bond that unites all Aspies is a strong feeling of alienation from the rest of the world.

In my own case that feeling is one I have felt very acutely at times, even when I was very young. As a child there was a very old Irish folk song that I used to love. The melody, like the melody of a lot of old Irish music, was beautiful and deeply moving. But it was the words that got to me.

Slievenamon
Alone, all alone,
On a wave-washed strand
And alone in a crowded hall
The hall it is gay
And the waves they are grand
But my heart is not here at all.

Charles Kickham

I remember feeling the meaning of those words very deeply – particularly the words 'alone in a crowded hall'. Those words resonated with me, because they reminded me of how I sometimes felt at my most alienated and alone when I was surrounded by people. Then later when I was a teenager I came across a French book called *L'Etranger* by Albert Camus, and I asked my sister, Deirdre, what the title meant. She told me it meant 'The Outsider' – and once again I had a deep feeling of recognition.

Years later I was on the internet investigating Asperger Syndrome. There were plenty of interesting websites to look at, but there was one that really stood out for me. It was called www.wrongplanet.net – once again it was the title that spoke to me. It summed up so neatly the bottom-line feeling of Asperger Syndrome, and the common bond that unites all those different and varied people under the one big umbrella.

You will come across this feeling of alienation in one form or another if you talk to Aspies or read autobiographies written by Aspies. And if you are an Aspie, you will recognise it yourself. The language may vary – sometimes people with AS say for example that they feel 'different', or 'like aliens', or that they 'don't belong'. But the feeling is the same. Aspies can always identify with that 'wrong planet' feeling, because that is how they feel a lot of the time.

And if they keep on saying the same thing, surely we need to take them seriously, for it is an important clue to understanding AS.

The common bond that unites all Aspies is a strong feeling of alienation from the rest of the world.

AN ASIDE

But before we go any further there is one thing I want to explain. I referred in the last paragraph to something that 'we' need to take seriously. And by 'we' what I really meant was NT's. But I have had a diagnosis of AS myself, so maybe you're wondering why I am identifying with NT's here rather than Aspies? I will try to explain.

Sometimes I find it very hard to organise myself – which is a trait of AS. This book has taken me probably 20 times more effort than it would have if that end of things hadn't been so hard. I really wanted to write it. All the ideas I wanted to express were in there –I just found them very hard to sort out and arrange. It felt a bit like trying to sort out a bag of knitting that the cat has been at; even if there are some lovely bits of patterns and balls of wool in there, it can be hard to pull them apart, or even to tell where one starts and another ends.

The ideas in my head were like that. Everything was tangled up and the knots were hard to undo. Sometimes when I tried too hard to organise my ideas, it got worse, in the same way as if you try to undo a knot by pulling, sometimes it just gets tighter.

It took a lot of time and effort to sort it all out. If I had to tell you all the different methods I tried, I would hardly know where to start. Quite a few times I was tempted to give up.

Probably the strategy that helped me most was to kind of stand apart from the Aspie part of myself and observe it. So I decided to write *from* my NT part *about* my Aspie part. It was the only way that seemed to work or to make sense for me.

YIN AND YANG

That brings us back to another important point, and one that is key to understanding Asperger Syndrome. All Aspies have their NT bits. And some Aspies are more Aspie than others, so to speak. The issue of categorising human beings can never be a black or white one. Maybe this is looking at it a bit simplistically, but there must be a cut off point where if someone has enough AS traits, then he is considered to 'have Asperger Syndrome' but if he doesn't have enough, then he is considered not to 'have Asperger Syndrome' (or, to put it in more official language, he has not 'satisfied the diagnostic criteria').

You can also look at it like this. Just as all Aspies have NT traits, in the same way, all NT's have 'Aspie traits', to some degree or other. The bottom line is this – there is nobody alive who is 100 per cent AS; and there is nobody alive who is 100 per cent NT.

You can picture this by using a 'yin and yang' type diagram something like this.

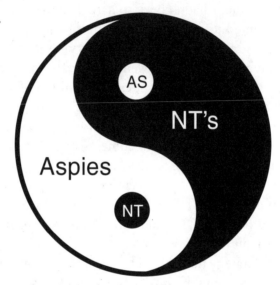

Figure 4.1 Yin and Yang. Here the relationship between AS and NT is simply illustrated. They are represented as opposing yet complementary aspects of human nature.

It is important that we realise this and keep this in mind. Here are some of the reasons:

- By acknowledging and owning more parts of ourselves, we have all a lot to learn about ourselves and each other.

- If we don't, we are at greater risk of putting people into boxes, thereby limiting and stereotyping them.

- Putting people rigidly into boxes is a bad thing, because it promotes feelings of division and separation between people, instead of encouraging us to remember all the things that we have in common.

- If NT's can acknowledge the Aspie parts of themselves it can help them to understand AS.

- If Aspies can acknowledge the NT parts of themselves it can help them understand how the NT world works. This should allow them to navigate it better and feel less isolated.

- Understanding the NT world can empower Aspies and help them overcome difficulties.

NOTHING NEW UNDER THE SUN

When Aspies say they feel like they are on the wrong planet and so forth, they are describing feelings that everyone in the world can recognise, so in this respect there is 'nothing new under the sun'.

We all know that feeling of alienation, for we have all felt it to some degree, at some time in our lives, but it is never a feeling that we welcome. It can be a depressing and scary feeling; yet ironically a lot of human misery comes as a result of efforts to avoid that feeling of alienation (for example by means of addictions – alcohol, drugs, overeating, over-busyness etc.).

It is said that for all human beings the number one fear is the fear of rejection. So perhaps the longing to avoid feelings of alienation lies at the root of more conformity than we realise. But people who do not conform can add to the richness of life and make remarkable contributions to humanity. Most of the greatest philosophers since the Greeks, for example, have not lived conventional lives or had normal family ties.

As with everything else about AS, the difference between it and so-called 'normality' is one of degree. Aspies feel the same thing, but they feel it more of the time, and to a more intense degree than most other people. The good news about that is that everyone can identify with the 'wrong planet' feelings.

In general, the best way for an NT to understand AS is to identify with the Aspie part of himself. But how does he do that in reality? It may at times simply mean that he acknowledges his own Aspie feelings, rather than denying them. Or he might choose to do or say something that makes him stand out from the crowd for some reason of his own – even when it makes him feel like a misfit.

ONUS ON NT'S

The bottom line is this – the best, and perhaps the only, way for NT's to understand AS is to take seriously what Aspies say about their feelings of alienation and to try to imagine what this might feel like and how it might affect their lives. The onus to do this is on NT's. Why? Because that ability to imagine and put yourself into the shoes of somebody else or to imagine how they might be feeling is, according to the experts, something Aspies find very difficult, but NT's find relatively easy.

That being the case it should not be too hard for an NT to imagine 'wrong planet' feelings – what they are like and what effect they might have. But imagination is like any other faculty – we can deliberately choose whether or not to exercise it.

How would you feel if you suddenly found yourself alone on the 'wrong planet', or in a foreign country, where you didn't know the language and you weren't familiar with the customs and culture? What words would you use to describe 'wrong planet' feelings?

I imagine they would be words like: alone, anxious, nervous, isolated, vulnerable, confused, isolated, homesick, lost, frustrated, frightened, tense.

When it comes to understanding AS, NT's can exercise their imagination by: (1) remembering times when they have felt 'wrong planet' feelings and then (2) asking themselves what it would be like to feel 'wrong planet' feelings much more deeply, acutely and frequently? I have provided some exercises for you to try on the following pages.

Exercise 1

Think of a situation or environment where you felt awkward or uncomfortable (e.g. a new environment, meeting a new person).

What happened?

How did this make you feel?

Exercise 2 .

Think of a time when you misinterpreted what someone said or did.

What happened?

How did this make you feel?

Exercise 3

Think of a time when you said something stupid or out of turn.

What happened?

How did this make you feel?

Exercise 4

Think of a time where you didn't have all the information you needed and so you got something wrong or felt confused.

What happened?

How did this make you feel?

A GOOD FIT?

If you really were on the 'wrong planet' or a visitor to a foreign country where you didn't know the language or customs, how would you appear to the natives? Would they notice anything strange about you? What effect might it have on how you behave?

It would probably affect you in three main areas:

1. **Anxiety:** You would show symptoms typical of anxiety.

2. **Behaviour:** Your behaviour might seem hard to understand or sometimes even challenging.

3. **Communication:** Another thing it would affect is how you communicate. You would probably find it very difficult to communicate with the 'natives'. And even if you did settle down and learn the language, you might always feel like an outsider, as if you didn't belong. No matter how long you stayed there, you might always seem to the natives too as if you didn't quite belong. You might always have the trace of a foreign accent, for example.

These three areas are common to people with Asperger Syndrome as well.

ASPERGER SYNDROME VS. WRONG PLANET SYNDROME – COMPARING THE 'SYMPTOMS'

Sometimes the 'symptoms' of AS seem very strange and mysterious, but if you think of AS as a kind of 'Wrong Planet Syndrome' it can start to make more sense. On the other hand we need to remember that this is only an analogy. Aspies are not aliens from a different planet, even if they do feel that way.

A good analogy will be one that fits reality well. So how well does this one fit? In order to find out, we will need to break down some of the main aspects and symptoms of AS and see how well they compare with the hypothetical symptoms of an imaginary alien or a foreign visitor who finds himself alone and unfamiliar with the local language, customs etc.

Just in case there is any misunderstanding, I should make it clear that by calling them 'symptoms', I am not implying that AS is some kind of illness. I am just using that word to help identify a list of the kind of things we can expect with AS.

Anxiety

IF YOU WERE AN ALIEN OR VISITOR

The fact that you were in an environment that you weren't used to would be enough to put you under stress and make you feel anxious.

COMPARING 'WRONG PLANET SYNDROME' WITH ASPERGER SYNDROME

A lot of the features of AS are consistent with anxiety, and rigidity is one example. When people are anxious they often find it harder than usual to be flexible and they may become more rigid. Again this is consistent with Asperger Syndrome.

For example:

- Everybody likes their routines and rituals. But when we are feeling anxious and under stress these can be even more important to us. Routines and rituals are very important to people with Asperger Syndrome.

- Quite a lot of people prefer to be left alone when they are anxious. Generally speaking, Aspies seem to find being with other people very stressful at times, and often need to be alone to unwind. They spend a lot of time on their own, to pursue their own interests and to think their own thoughts.

- When we are anxious we can become inflexible, bossy and controlling. Again this is something we see a lot in Aspies.

- To relieve our anxiety we may find something time-consuming and absorbing to do. Aspies do this a lot when they throw themselves into their special interests or obsessions.

■ We are more likely to be intolerant of little things not going our way, and to come across as perfectionist. Again this is an Aspie trait.

Behaviour

IF YOU WERE AN ALIEN OR VISITOR
You might behave in ways that seemed odd or eccentric – perhaps simply because you didn't know quite how you were supposed to behave. Sometimes if you were frustrated enough – through trying to cope with a foreign language, get to grips with local customs and the local way of life – you might even throw a tantrum (i.e. exhibit 'bad' behaviour).

COMPARING 'WRONG PLANET SYNDROME' WITH ASPERGER SYNDROME
Aspies often exhibit a lot of behaviour that appears odd and eccentric, as well as so-called 'bad behaviour'. (I know these days it is not politically correct to talk about behaviour being 'bad' and people prefer to call it demanding or challenging behaviour. So I'll put it this way. Whatever name you give it, the kind of behaviour that used to be called 'bad behaviour' is often a symptom of AS.)

Communication

IF YOU WERE AN ALIEN OR VISITOR
You would not know the local language, so you would not be able to communicate very well with the locals. You could take formal lessons and learn, but your accent might always make you seem different. This could make it hard for you to feel accepted or properly integrated.

COMPARING 'WRONG PLANET SYNDROME' WITH ASPERGER SYNDROME
For Aspies the equivalent of 'local customs and culture' lies largely in non-verbal communication, for that is the main area of communication that is foreign to them. This may manifest in many ways. For example Aspies can sometimes:

- be insensitive to non-verbal unwritten rules and assumptions (e.g. rules that state what topics are appropriate to talk about, and in what circumstances, and with whom)

- not understand the concept of hierarchies (an Aspie child may talk to the headmaster in exactly the same way as he talks to the other children)

- not understand the concept of team games

- be seen as tactless

- not be conversant with figures of speech and tend to take what people say very literally

- not pick up on subtle nuances that would help them understand the motivation of other people – which can make them very vulnerable

- not be skilful with the unwritten rules of conversation such as:

  o people take turns at talking

  o long silences in conversations make other people feel uncomfortable

  o people do not like to listen to long monologues – especially about subjects that are of little interest to them.

Other subtle differences and problems

IF YOU WERE AN ALIEN OR VISITOR
There may be subtle things about you which, though hard to pinpoint, nevertheless set you apart and make you feel different.

COMPARING 'WRONG PLANET SYNDROME' WITH ASPERGER SYNDROME
Aspies seem different, for example, when they:

- display unusual areas of skill, for example computer skills

- have unusual memory skills

- display unusual areas of difficulty and have some specific learning problems

- generally seem 'out of sync' with everyone else around them.

SUMMING UP

Overall, the 'wrong planet' analogy fits very well. It serves to confirm the underlying truth – that feelings of alienation are extremely common among people with AS and must go some way to account for its typical 'symptoms' and traits. And because everyone suffers from feelings of alienation to some extent, this insight makes AS a bit easier to understand.

But if Aspies feel like aliens, visitors or misfits, then there must be something going on that they are missing out on. What is that?

In the next chapter we will begin to find out.

Chapter 5

THE DECODING APPROACH

CODE:

A system of accepted laws and regulations that govern procedure or behaviour.

Encarta English Dictionary

What is the Social Code? Here are some of the things we know about it.

- It is large and complex.

- It contains social 'laws' that govern how people in society behave towards each other.

- Most of society follows it without even knowing they are doing it.

- It is important, for it keeps social interactions between people running smoothly (most of the time anyway).

- Although it consists of verbal and non-verbal rules, most of the problems that Aspies have are with the non-verbal rules.

According to the experts, one of the reasons why Asperger Syndrome causes so many difficulties is that Aspies often break the Social Code. That being the case, if we can really get to grips with it, that should provide us with another key that can help us understand Asperger Syndrome.

So let's look into some basic questions:

1. How 'real' is the Social Code?

2. Who keeps it and who breaks it?

3. Are there any penalties if the code gets broken, and if so what are they?

4. How can the Decoding Approach help us deal with Asperger Syndrome in a more positive way?

1. HOW REAL IS THE SOCIAL CODE?

There are many kinds of laws in the world, and it is easy to think of social laws as being less important and less 'real' than other laws. But when we do that, we are inclined to take social laws less seriously. So it is worth comparing social laws with other types of law, to analyse where the similarities and differences lie, in order to see how 'real' the Social Code actually is.

Comparing social laws, gravity and red lights

Looking at it in a very general way, laws are rules or statements that dictate how things run in the world, or set out what is generally taken to be true or binding. So social laws are real at least in this sense – they dictate how things run in the social world.

Let's compare social laws with two other types of law: (1) the law of gravity and (2) the law of the road, by holding each of them up against various criteria: (a) Source; (b) Rigidity; (c) How we know them; (d) Purpose; (e) Complexity; (f) Obviousness.

(A) SOURCE (SCIENTIFIC VS. MAN-MADE)

Gravity is a law of science, and as such it dictates what normally happens in the physical world; but you don't need to be a scientist to know basically what it says. At its simplest level, as we all know, it states that apples fall to the ground; they don't float in the sky!

Traffic law is not a law of science, but nevertheless it is a real law in that it dictates what normally happens on the road. To take a simple example, when we are driving and we come to a red light we stop. Some time somewhere, people must have agreed that this would be the case. Presumably it was an arbitrary decision at the time, in the sense that they could have decided that red lights meant 'go' just as easily as deciding that red lights meant 'stop'.

We recognise and accept both of these very different examples as real laws. But what about social laws?

While the law of gravity is a law of physics, and laws of the road are man-made, social laws have elements of both.

(B) RIGID VS. FLEXIBLE?

Unlike traffic laws, there was never a specific time that people sat down and decided that social laws would be as they are. The process of how they came to be agreed is a bit mysterious, and it would seem that they evolved. But they are not rigid and definite like the laws of physical science.

Because it is a physical law it is impossible to 'break' the law of gravity. It just is what it is – the laws of science must be obeyed, whereas man-made laws do not necessarily.

So in that sense social laws are more like traffic laws than physical laws.

(C) KNOWN THROUGH OBSERVATION

In the case of both traffic laws and scientific laws, we can conclude that they exist by observation. We see time and again what normally happens in the physical world; and we see time and again what happens on the road.

Social laws are laws in the same way – although obviously some people find it easier than others to know them through observation!

(D) OBVIOUSLY PURPOSEFUL?

It's easy to see the point of physical laws. They are what keep the physical world turning over. Traffic laws are also easy to see the point of – they keep the traffic running smoothly. Not all man-made laws are like that though. Some are harder than others to see the point of.

Social laws can be hard to see the point of as well – to people with Asperger Syndrome in particular.

(E) COMPLEX VS. STRAIGHTFORWARD?

Social laws are arguably more complex and hard to tie down than either physical or traffic laws, because they are subject to a fair bit of what you might call local variation. In other words, the laws about what is expected are not completely consistent or predictable. Social laws change depending on many circumstances and it would be very hard, if not impossible, for anyone to itemise exactly what all these circumstances might be.

(F) SUBTLE OR OBVIOUS?

Usually in practice the only time we are really aware of social laws is when they get broken. We may not know exactly what law has been broken. All that we know is that something does not feel right. If someone says or does something that we find rude or offensive, unless it is very blatant, usually we are just left with a vague impression that it felt 'rude' but we may not be able to put our finger on exactly how. We are just left with a vague feeling of discomfort, annoyance, irritation, frustration, outrage or anger.

Traffic laws are obvious. Gravity is not (at least not until it is pointed out to you!) but as a law of science it is impossible to break.

Social laws are easy to break and can be very subtle. So subtle in fact that when they are broken, sometimes even NT's are not quite sure what they are.

2. THE SOCIAL CODE – WHO KEEPS IT AND WHO BREAKS IT?

The short answer to the question 'Who keeps the Social Code?' is basically 'Most people keep it most of the time.'

And when you think about it that can seem harder to understand than why some people sometimes break it! The Social Code is so complex that it is amazing most people even know what it is. Yet usually they follow it pretty well without even thinking about it.

And the short answer to the question 'Who breaks the Social Code?' is very often as simple as this: 'People who don't get it'.

There are a few categories of people whom we expect to break the Social Code because it is obvious that they 'don't get it' – children and foreign visitors for example.

Little children are well known for breaking the laws of the Social Code. For instance they tell the truth even when it's embarrassing. Let's take a very simple example. Aunty Lily has come to visit. A little child might blurt out to her that she shouldn't have any more ice cream because she's already 'far too fat'. That is the sort of thing we expect from a small child, and we are inclined to be tolerant and to allow for it.

And we expect foreign visitors to break social rules from time to time. Visitors to London for example, may not realise that there is an unwritten rule requiring pedestrians to keep to a particular side of the walkway when using the underground.

Usually we don't take too much offence when visitors or children break the Social Code. We make allowances for foreign visitors, and we laugh at little children, when they make social gaffes. On the other hand, we expect foreign visitors to gradually adapt to our culture, and we expect children to be become more socially skilled as they grow up – which generally speaking they do. As they get older children learn more about what is appropriate and what is not appropriate for them to say and do. The adults around them have to give them guidance here and there, but a lot of it they just seem to 'pick up'. This is part of the natural process of social maturity.

The basic reason why people are tolerant of social gaffes from children and foreign visitors is that they *realise* they do not know what is expected and so they mean no harm. But there is another category of people who are liable to break social laws – people who have Asperger Syndrome. And unfortunately when they do, it is a different story.

Take the example of the comment to Aunty Lily – that might seem funny if it comes from a young child, but if it comes from an older child or an adult it would probably be taken as rude and offensive. The world is less tolerant of Aspies than of either foreign visitors or little children, for there is no reason why an Aspie should not know social laws and conform to them – no reason that is obvious to the world anyway.

3. ARE THERE ANY PENALTIES IF THE CODE GETS BROKEN, AND IF SO WHAT ARE THEY?

It is tough on the Aspie and on the people around him when he causes offence by breaking laws he didn't know existed. The Social Code is like a real law in one important sense – there are penalties for breaking it.

If I was to tell you that there were a set of new laws being introduced tomorrow that would affect your life on a daily basis, but I didn't tell you what they were, would you like it? I guess not. What if I then told you that any time you broke one of these laws you would run the risk of being penalised? I imagine you would think that was pretty unfair.

Yet that is what happens to Aspies. They are continually breaking rules and being penalised, even though they may have only the dimmest awareness of what these rules are or how or when they are breaking them.

The penalties for breaking 'the laws' (civil and criminal) may be argued to be fair or unfair, but at least they are usually clear. Social laws are often unclear, and the penalties hard to predict or detect. They may range from mild to severe. Penalties may be anything from bullying, ridicule, isolation or rejection, which in turn can lead to a vicious cycle of lost confidence, academic and social failure, boredom and depression.

4. THE DECODING APPROACH

In order to deal with Asperger Syndrome in a more positive way, we need first and foremost to see the Social Code as a real code, and take it seriously, just as we would any other code. Going back for a moment to the 'Wrong Planet' analogy – what would be the fair thing to do if an alien or visitor kept breaking laws and regulations? The first thing would surely be to make sure he was aware of them and if necessary to inform him, break the code down clearly and explain it to him.

If NT's could decode social rules and expectations for Aspies it would help make life a lot easier. But before they could explain the Social Code they would need to: (1) acknowledge that there is a code and (2) identify exactly what it is. (That incidentally can be a useful exercise for NT's to do, because the Social Code is often followed without question; it can be challenging and interesting to bring social laws and conventions to light and assess them.)

Once social laws are identified, NT's and Aspies can then decide whether they think they are a good idea. It is good to bring these things into the open and challenge them. Identifying them is useful from the point of view of the Aspie as well, because he can then see clearly where he has gone 'wrong'. That makes it easier for him to make a more informed choice and decision – to modify his behaviour or not as the case may be.

EXPLAINING THE DECODING APPROACH

When the Social Code is taken seriously, it can be a helpful way of thinking about and understanding AS. 'The Decoding Approach' can then be used as a positive approach, rather than a practical strategy (of course it can be used in conjunction with practical strategies).

When there is a problem, a simple template can be used to help break it down – something like this for example:

THE DECODING APPROACH – A TEMPLATE

What happened?	How was this offensive?	What aspect(s) of the Social Code have been broken?

The Decoding Approach can be broken down into 10 steps as follows:

step 1. accept and acknowledge that social laws exist

step 2. identify what they are

step 3. communicate clearly to Aspies what they are

step 4. (ideally) be honest with themselves about whether these rules matter and if so why

step 5. (ideally) communicate this clearly to Aspies as well

step 6. acknowledge when and where it is that they are penalising Aspies.

And Aspies in their turn need to:

step 7. be open to learning about the Social Code

step 8. be prepared to try to remember it and apply it, and

step 9. be realistic about the fact that it will often be difficult to learn, and may take a long time

step 10. Then NT's need to appreciate the efforts that Aspies make to fit in as well as they do.

Decoding – an example

If you have encountered AS at all, you will be very familiar with how things 'go wrong' when the Social Code is broken. Practical examples are easy to find, and there are plenty of practical strategies that can be helpful. Just to illustrate the principle, let me give you a very simple example of The Decoding Approach in practice. (It is based on a real example, but real names are not used.)

Here is the scenario:

Michael is five years old. Every day after school his Dad collects him and drives him home. On their way home, they often have to call and collect Michael's old Aunt Maria and give her a lift as well. Michael likes to sit in the front seat of the car. Every time Dad asks him to get out of the front seat and move into the back seat so that Aunt Maria can get into the front, Michael refuses and causes a scene, sometimes throwing a tantrum. Dad doesn't know how to handle this, and he has tried various approaches, including shouting and punishing (e.g. not allowing Michael to watch his favourite TV programme).

Let's look at how The Decoding Approach might help in this situation.

THE DECODING APPROACH – USING THE TEMPLATE

What happened?	How was this offensive?	What aspect(s) of the Social Code have been broken?
Michael refused to get into the back seat.	1. Dad was embarrassed. 2. Aunt Maria was inconvenienced.	When children and adults are travelling in the car, children normally sit in the back and adults in the front. (It is regarded as rude for children to refuse to get into the back.)

If we analyse it more closely, we could perhaps use the ten steps as follows:

step 1. Dad accepts and acknowledges that the Social Code exists.

step 2. He identifies the law that is causing the problem. The Decoding Approach is not an exact science of course, but often it is quite easy to identify social laws. The social law in question here could be stated fairly simply – perhaps something like this:

When children and adults are travelling in the car, it is good manners for the children to sit in the back and allow the adults to sit in the front. Or perhaps: *When children and adults are travelling in the car, it is seen as rude for children not to get in the back.*

step 3. It is best if Dad gives Michael plenty of notice, and tries The Decoding Approach at a time when Michael is likely to be receptive – the night before for example. And ideally he will tell him in a calm, unemotional way – as if he is giving him some interesting information rather than telling him what to do and where he is going wrong.

step 4. Dad will handle it best if he asks himself the reason for this particular Social Rule.

step 5. Sometimes there is a good reason for a social rule. If there is, Dad might explain to Michael, for example, that Aunt Maria finds it a bit tricky to get in and out of the car. But sometimes when you analyse it, certain aspects of the Social Code are just plain daft! If Dad can see the funny side and the two of them have a laugh about it, that can be very positive and helpful.

step 6. Dad acknowledges that he has been penalising Michael by shouting and punishing him (and determines to try 'Social Decoding' before penalising him when there are similar problems in future).

step 7. Michael needs to be open to learning about the Social Code; and

step 8. Be prepared to try to remember it and apply it.

    (Both these will be more likely if there is a good, trusting relationship between Dad and Michael – and if Dad picks a good time to talk to him about the Social Code!)

step 9. In this example, the Social Code is easy and straightforward, so that Michael may learn and remember it easily. But many social laws are much more subtle and complex. Teaching and learning these can take great patience from Dad and perseverance from Michael. (On the bright side, AS parents are often patient, and AS children are often persistent!)

step 10. Ideally Dad will appreciate the efforts that Michael has made, and pass some positive comment to let Michael know he has noticed, when (it is hoped) he makes the effort to remember and apply the Social Code by letting Aunt Maria in the front seat of the car.

Obviously in real life, there will rarely be time to do an in-depth analysis like this when an Aspie breaks a social law. But the Decoding Approach can always be used as a way of thinking at least.

An exercise

Next time you encounter a problem, use the template below and try the Decoding Approach.

What happened?	How was this offensive?	What aspect(s) of the Social Code have been broken?

Chapter 6

LABELS AND BOXES

Whatever way we look at it, we need to acknowledge that Asperger Syndrome is a kind of label – and some people have a real problem with the very idea of labelling people. This chapter outlines some of the main arguments surrounding this topic – so if the issue of labelling is not of interest to you, please feel free to skip over it!

THE PROBLEMS WITH LABELS

Only a few generations ago there was 'no such thing' as AS in the sense that it was not recognised as a condition in its own right. But Aspies have always been with us – they just didn't have the label AS before. When there is a diagnosis in the family it is quite common to hear family members talk about older relations who were very similar, and who probably would be diagnosed if they were assessed today.

A syndrome is a kind of label, and even though AS is not new, the label is. But is it overall a good thing that we have a label called AS – especially when it is so wide-ranging that it covers everything from autism to giftedness?

Some aspects of Asperger behaviour can be difficult and challenging to other people. Often when people meet typical Asperger behaviour, they find it extremely challenging. It is acknowledged that many people with Asperger Syndrome can come across as rude, gauche, arrogant, unfriendly and uncooperative. People they come up against can react with avoidance or even aggression, understandably enough. This kind of thing takes its toll on the individual with Asperger Syndrome, and can leave him more socially isolated than he would otherwise be.

If, on the other hand, people are aware that he has a 'syndrome' it can be something of an advantage. If they know that any difficult Asperger behaviour is neither personal nor intentional, their reaction should be less negative.

THE ASPERGER LABEL

There are two main problems with the label AS and they are: (1) the negative connotations of some of the words that are used, and (2) stereotyping.

The power of words

Words are important, and some words are loaded with hard-wired con- notations – the word syndrome, for example. It carries association with illness, disability, disadvantage and inferiority – associations that are clearly far from positive. What do you automatically think of when you hear the word syndrome? Does it sound to you like a medical term? I think that most people would say yes. It brings to mind a medical condi- tion of some sort.

Being labelled with Asperger Syndrome can play into the individ- ual's basic human fears – fear that I'm not OK, fear that there is something 'wrong' with me, fear of rejection etc. Imagine you have felt different all your life. You have struggled to fit in and suffered a lot of misunderstanding, judgement and isolation. At last you are offered an explanation. You 'have Asperger Syndrome'. What does that mean? It is not an illness in the usual way. You are not going to die of it. But you are not going to be cured of it either.

How would it affect you if the very essence of who you are turns out to be a medical condition, one that needs to be formally diagnosed? Not only a medical condition, but also some form of disability?

Stereotyping

Another problem is that when we apply a label like Asperger Syndrome to someone it is very easy to stereotype and put him or her in a box, so to speak. And when we put people in boxes we insult and limit them. It can be tempting to think, just because we have learned a little bit about Asperger Syndrome, that we know more than we really do and make assumptions instead of treating each Aspie as an individual. We need to remember that the individual is far greater than any label we may place on him.

Parents are very often reluctant to 'label' their children, and this is one of the reasons they give. They don't like the idea that outsiders might stereotype them. I can understand this, because it is one of the things that I used to tell myself, and it held me back from seeking a diagnosis for my own son. I was afraid that not only would he be 'labelled' but that somehow the act of putting a label on him would make his condition worse and encourage him to live up to the stereotype. In the end I came to realise that this was not the case.

Another problem with stereotyping is that it can provide ammunition to mean-spirited people to treat the individual concerned with conde-scension rather than to make allowances.

THE ADVANTAGES OF LABELS

But there are advantages to labels and in particular to the label 'AS.' These are: (1) Classification; (2) Communication; (3) Practical benefits.

Classification

The main purpose of labels in general is that they are a means of classifi-cation, and classification is essential. It helps us to communicate – or rather to know what it is we are communicating about. If there were no generally accepted classification of trees, for example, how would you know what I meant when I talked to you about, say, a lime tree as opposed to an oak?

Theoretically, I suppose I could describe the lime tree to you in enough detail for you to know what kind of tree I meant. But being able to classify it as a lime tree is a helpful kind of shorthand that saves me the trouble of doing that.

It is a bit the same with Asperger Syndrome. If there were no such classification it would be much harder to group together and identify people who meet the classification criteria – because there wouldn't be such a criteria!

Communication

Without the classification that we call Asperger Syndrome, people who were interested in the condition (or whatever you would call it) would have very few means of connecting with each other. Ideas, insights and breakthroughs could not be shared in the way they currently are and it would be much harder to make progress. All this would be a great loss.

So the classification in itself has had this benefit anyway. By facilitating people to connect and communicate with each other about a shared interest, it has played a major role in the huge rise in awareness, understanding and tolerance about AS that has taken place over the last few decades.

It has also provided an avenue for people with AS themselves to connect with each other, if that is what they want to do. And for people with Aspergers this can be a big advantage, because they are often isolated and feel different from the so-called 'normal' people around them. It can be a great relief to be able to connect with like-minded people.

Practical benefits

In practical terms, being labelled with Asperger Syndrome should encourage a more helpful response from outsiders.

Another advantage in practical terms is that if you are diagnosed with a recognised syndrome, this is usually interpreted to mean that you have a recognised disability. As such, you should be able to take advantage of anti-discrimination legislation, for example in employment. And it can open certain doors to help and services from social services, medical and education authorities.

Attitudes to labels

These days, people are generally able to get a diagnosis at a younger age than used to be the case. This means, I hope, that in the future there will be fewer people having to wait till well into adulthood before they get the chance to really understand the cause of the difficulties they have coped with for so long. But even when a child receives a diagnosis when he is young, there is always an in-between period before diagnosis, when it is obvious that there is something 'different' about him, but it is not clear what or why.

Going along the road of assessment can be a big decision which an adult needs to make for himself. But when a child is displaying symptoms of Asperger Syndrome, parents are often reluctant to go along the road of assessment. They may believe or hope that over time the child will grow out of his difficulties.

Diagnosis can seem like such an important answer and explanation at any age however, and Aspies can be very sensitive to how other people respond to the diagnosis. An Aspie sees AS as an important part of his identity, don't forget, and so if he feels that people around him do not like the label, he may interpret this as meaning they do not like him.

Sometimes people say that it is not Asperger Syndrome that they don't like; it is the very idea of labelling that they are against. And some parents reject the idea that their child may have AS on the basis that they don't like the idea of labelling any child, full stop. But this may not be the real truth.

What people usually mean when they say they don't like labels is really that they don't like *certain* labels, rather than labels in general. If we are honest, we can all admit that there are some labels we admire and are proud of, and others that we are not so keen on.

GIFTED – A NICER LABEL?

The truth of this came home to me quite graphically once when my son was small. I was still at the stage of not knowing what was 'wrong' and exploring every avenue I could think of to try and find out. But I had still never heard of Asperger Syndrome.

Some of Kenneth's teachers had noticed that even though he was very withdrawn in school, he had read every book in the library at great speed. Also, he rarely did any of the work that he was supposed to do, but he showed an interest the odd time when there was something interesting or complicated going on in maths. And he seemed to find difficult maths very easy. His teacher knew that academically gifted children often have problems because they are bored and don't fit in at school and she suggested that perhaps his problem was that he was gifted. He was tested and the results showed that he did come within the official definition of giftedness. And for a while I was very happy with this label as an explanation.

But before too long I came to realise that the label of giftedness was no help to him. Months went by, but despite the best efforts of everyone concerned, his problems continued to get worse. Someone suggested that maybe he had some form of high functioning autism, but I closed my ears and got him enrolled in NAGC (National Association for Gifted Children). I began to take him to local NAGC children's events, but before long it was obvious that nothing had changed.

There was a little girl in the NAGC club who drew my attention. I only saw her a few times and I didn't know the family at all, but there was something about her that appealed to me. At first I didn't know what. Then it came to me. She reminded me of Kenneth, and she seemed to have almost exactly the same difficulties that he had.

One day I overheard her Mum talk. She was very concerned because apparently the school psychologists were trying to say there was something 'wrong' with her little girl – they were trying to say she had Asperger Syndrome!

'I'm not saying I have anything against Asperger Syndrome,' I remember her saying. 'It's just that I'm totally against putting labels on children.'

Looking back I can see that this for me was one of those defining moments. The irony was obvious. How could she say she didn't like labels? For what is 'gifted' if not a label?

The truth was not so much that she was against labels, but that there were some labels she was more comfortable with than others. And 'gifted' seemed like a much nicer label than 'Asperger Syndrome'.

In that moment I knew in my heart that the same was true for me. And I made a fundamental decision. I was going to open my mind and find out the whole truth about my son. I suddenly knew it was the right thing, even if it meant putting on a label that I wasn't that comfortable with!

Chapter 7

GETTING IT RIGHT

How do we make sure that the AS label is correctly applied? If we think of Asperger Syndrome as being like a big umbrella (see Chapter 3), then how do we make sure the wrong people don't come under it? How, come to that, do we make sure the right people do come under it?

There is a certain safeguard against the wrong people coming under the AS umbrella in that the process of formal diagnosis is fairly stringent. Speculation is easy, but to be officially diagnosed, you need to be assessed by an expert who is qualified to give such a diagnosis – and the expert needs to be satisfied that certain very specific things are true about you. All of this is designed to be as precise as possible. Diagnostic criteria have been agreed so that there is little room for inconsistency, so that, in other words, what is called AS is the same in each part of the world. The formal process of diagnosis therefore helps prevent the 'wrong' people coming under the umbrella.

But there is no such mechanism to ensure that the 'right' people do come under the umbrella – or even to encourage them to do so.

HIDDEN ASPIES

AS diagnosis is on the increase these days. But there are still bound to be 'hidden Aspies' out there.

Aspies can be 'hidden' in either of the following ways:

- **Secret diagnosis**: Some people who get a diagnosis decide, for whatever reason, to keep it to themselves, so that the rest of the world never finds out about it.

- **Under-diagnosis**: People who would satisfy the diagnostic criteria never actually go for assessment.

There seems to be no doubt that there are 'hidden Aspies' in the world, but naturally it is impossible to know how many.

Understanding the phenomenon

People who are officially diagnosed with Asperger Syndrome are liable to receive the shelter and advantages of the 'AS umbrella', which will, it is hoped include some entitlement to recognition, understanding and support. So if there are certain benefits to coming under the AS umbrella, why do Aspies resist diagnosis in the first place?

Under-diagnosis must partly be due to lack of awareness. And sometimes when people want to keep their diagnosis secret, there is no other reason except that they think it is a personal matter. But sometimes it is because attitudes to AS are somewhat negative, in that Asperger Syndrome is perceived as, to put it bluntly, an unpopular condition.

Do people feel negative about AS? If so, they are rarely going to admit it in so many words. But there is one fairly reliable way of finding out how people really feel, and that is to have a look at their attitudes to diagnosis. And in my experience people are rarely delighted about it.

ATTITUDES TO DIAGNOSIS

I have been privileged, over the course of the last ten years or so, through my involvement in the world of Asperger Syndrome, to talk to many people who either have Asperger Syndrome, or else have a family member (or members) with a diagnosis. Sometimes when I talk to them the diagnosis is still very new, and in these situations I notice that they seem to feel a lot of the same feelings that I felt when my own son was first diagnosed. There can be a complex and wide range of emotions involved, sometimes including sadness, shock, confusion and guilt.

There may also be some element of relief for the fact that the end of a difficult and perplexing road has been reached, and an explanation found at last.

On the plus side, people see that there is a lot to be said for knowing there is a name and explanation for the problems they have been having, that there really are other people in the world who are in a similar position, and that there is help available.

But apart from that, the news of a diagnosis is rarely received as something to celebrate. AS in the family is rarely seen as good news. And I have seen this trend in the general public and in professionals as well.

Sometimes when I see families it is quite some time after the diagnosis, so that they have had plenty of time to 'get used' to it. These families naturally seem to be more comfortable with the diagnosis and all that it entails. But no matter what stage things are at when I talk to families, I am not sure I have ever met anyone who had a genuinely and unreservedly positive attitude to Asperger Syndrome.

And I have to admit I was no different myself. When I first got my diagnosis I had very mixed feelings and for quite some time I didn't want anyone to know about it. Partly that was because I needed time to process the information and get used to it myself, but if I am truthful about it, it was partly because I didn't like the idea of being labelled with Asperger Syndrome.

I have seen this kind of cynical attitude all too often in people with Asperger Syndrome. Not only in adults and adolescents, but also in quite young children. Parents often talk about how their children reach a stage where they honestly wish they had never heard of AS – even in cases where they initially accepted the diagnosis well. All too often the self-esteem takes a terrible battering. They feel like misfits. Aspies often desperately want just to be 'normal' and prefer to deny and disown their Asperger Syndrome.

If we want to try and turn this trend around, it is important that we acknowledge it and try and understand why it has come about.

A vicious cycle

The Asperger umbrella is a very large one, as we have seen. It includes people who have obvious significant problems and those who have more subtle difficulties. But in reality, even when people know about AS, they are very unlikely to go for assessment unless they have had some fairly significant problems.

Generally speaking Asperger Syndrome has a more negative image than it deserves, and there is a kind of vicious cycle about diagnosis that helps explain this.

Here's a broad picture of how it all seems to fit together:

1. AS has a negative image in the first place, making people in general reluctant to associate with it. Therefore Aspies who can manage without diagnosis are more likely to do so (i.e. ones who seem to have fewer problems).

2. Most people who get diagnosed with AS will have gone for assessment because they had significant problems of some sort, and the diagnosis serves as some kind of an explanation for them. At school, for example, the kind of Aspies who are more likely to be diagnosed are the ones who are at the more extreme end of difficulty – for example a child who is exhibiting more extreme behaviour problems.

3. The overall picture of AS becomes distorted and misleading – 'problem' Aspies are over-represented.

4. After diagnosis people are keen to find out more about AS, which includes trying to get help with certain problems. So they seek out information from books, the internet, etc. The information they find out is very helpful, but often has a lot of focus on the problem side of AS (which is inevitable, for you cannot suggest a solution to a problem unless you first identify what that problem is!).

5. These things foster the generally negative impression about AS.

6. Insofar as AS has a negative image:

   ○ people who are diagnosed with AS are less likely to feel good about themselves

◦   some people who may have AS are put off coming forward for diagnosis.

7. The people who are most likely to come forward for diagnosis are those for whom AS is more of a problem.

8. The negative image is reinforced (and so back to No. 1).

Getting it right

If we were really getting things right, then:

- Aspies would be proud and happy about who they are, not embarrassed and ashamed.

- People who have been diagnosed would be less likely to keep it secret.

- More hidden Aspies who have never been diagnosed would come forward for assessment.

Know thyself

It is hard to know how many hidden Aspies there are in the world but there may be a lot more than we would imagine, and it is a great shame to think that people feel they need to hide parts of themselves.

Ancient wisdom gives us this piece of advice 'Know thyself': It suggests that the route to wisdom and happiness lies in inner searching so as to find our true identity. Knowing ourselves of course means knowing *all* of ourselves. That's the hard bit, for there are always some parts of ourselves that we are happier to know than others.

In order for a person with AS to really know himself, he too needs to know all of himself – and that includes the AS part. In fact the AS part may be the most important part of all. How easy or difficult will he find it to accept those parts of himself? It all depends on how positive or negative his attitude to AS is.

When someone has Asperger Syndrome, then this is an important and intrinsic part of his identity. Ideally a diagnosis should be an interesting, helpful, even a positive, description that helps us understand a person. Something is going wrong if it is seen as some kind of stigma.

The important thing is this. When a person has AS, all those things about him that make him AS are very much part of him and he is not going to change. Yes, you can work out ways to modify behaviour and tackle things differently; we do have certain choices in life. But essentially we cannot change who we are, even if we wanted to. So when we tell someone he has AS we are providing at least part of the answer to the most important question of all – Who am I? That is why we need to tread very carefully.

On a brighter note, awareness about AS has grown at a phenomenal rate over the last generation or so. You only have to go on-line (or check out Jessica Kinglsey Publishers' book-list!) to see evidence of this. That must be at least part of the reason that the rate of diagnosis is increasing. And not all attitudes to AS are negative. Some people who have AS are proud of it. I spoke to a lot of Aspies while I was writing this book who said that they felt proud of their AS; and even that AS was the most positive thing about them (see Aspie Quotations at the back of this book).

WHO ARE HIDDEN ASPIES LIKELY TO BE?

Presumably one of the reasons why people resist diagnosis is that they associate AS with autism and disability. But there is another very different thing that AS is associated with and that is giftedness. These days we hear a lot about people with exceptional brains, creativity and talent who are said to have Asperger Syndrome, both in our world today and throughout history. How common is that connection? Again, it is hard to say, but it may be more common than we realise.

There may be quite a few hidden Aspies who are gifted, and the reason they stay hidden is partly because of negative attitudes. The net result of the vicious cycle we looked at above is that more able people with fewer problems, even if they do have AS, are less likely to come forward. This may mean that there are more highly able and gifted Aspies than we realise who are 'hidden'.

It is fascinating as well as confusing that AS can be associated on the one hand with autism and on the other hand with certain types of giftedness or brilliance. Autism is generally perceived as some form of disability and mental illness. So if AS is a form of autism, how come some fantastically gifted people are said to have it? This is confusing as well as fascinating. Is there some truth, we ask ourselves, in the old saying that genius is next to madness? No wonder people find it intriguing!

So where does the truth lie in all this? In the next three chapters we will try to get to the bottom of it. In the next chapter we will look at the phenomenon of hidden Aspies from a personal point of view, and then in Chapters 9 and 10 we will look at the connections between AS and autism on one hand and AS and giftedness on the other.

Chapter 8

THE WILDERNESS YEARS

Just to recap on where we have got to so far as regards hidden Aspies: we have identified the phenomenon and had a look at the likely extent and possible reasons for it. But the reasons we have looked at have been quite general ones. What might go on at a more personal level when someone is a hidden Aspie? What effect might it have on his or her life? Obviously I am in a position to give a deeper, more personal insight on this from my own experience, so in this chapter I will tell you a bit about my life as a 'hidden Aspie' – the years I look back on now as my 'wilderness years'.

As far as I can tell, my experience as a hidden Aspie is quite similar to the experience of other hidden Aspies. There are certainly a lot of common features. These features are:

1. Denial and procrastination.

2. Other people's suspicions.

3. Noticing specific traits.

4. Diagnosis in the close family.

5. 'Crazy' decisions.

6. Background feelings.

7. Wearing a mask and/or learning to fit in.

8. Coming to terms and acceptance.

COMMON FEATURE 1: DENIAL AND PROCRASTINATION

When you think about it, it is strange that it took me such a long time to get a diagnosis for myself, especially when I was so much involved in the world of Asperger Syndrome. It was just one of those things that I kept putting off until I could put it off no more. Even though I was prepared to see myself as an Asperger Mum and to explore it and write about it, I was not prepared to own up to it in myself.

But why? The easiest way to explain this would be to say that I was 'in denial'. If someone is in denial it means there is something he or she doesn't want to know, so for a long time clearly I must not have wanted to know I had Asperger Syndrome – or maybe I was just not ready to know.

COMMON FEATURE 2: OTHER PEOPLE'S SUSPICIONS

And did the people around me know? That's a hard one to answer. It's always hard to tell how other people really see you, so I am not sure whether other people noticed anything unusual about me that would have made them think I had Asperger Syndrome.

Before I was diagnosed, people who knew about AS used to joke with me quite a lot about how they wouldn't be surprised if I had AS myself, but because I wasn't ready to really face the possibility, I didn't take them seriously and of course they didn't push it. In spite of that, when I did finally get my diagnosis I was surprised at people's reactions. When I finally plucked up the courage to tell some people, very few of them were really surprised.

COMMON FEATURE 3: NOTICING SPECIFIC TRAITS

What was life like for me as an Aspie without a diagnosis 'pretending to be normal'? That's a hard one to answer as well, because to some extent we all just accept our circumstances in life without questioning them too much. 'Each man appears orthodox unto himself' as they say.

There were some very specific traits which, looking back now, make it seem more obvious. But it is easy to see AS traits as just part of your personality. For example, I have always felt like a bit of a misfit, but I was used to that feeling; I had become very skilful at adopting roles and doing a good job of at least seeming to fit in. I hated certain social events and liked to have a lot of time alone. I was very determined and obsessive, and prone to depression.

But I was very determined to overcome any aspect of my personality that I felt was 'negative'. You could even say I was obsessed by that drive – and if there was any aspect I couldn't overcome, I was determined to hide it.

COMMON FEATURE 4: DIAGNOSIS IN THE CLOSE FAMILY

When I was younger I had never even heard of AS, but as soon as my son was diagnosed, I could see that there was a lot of it in me too. And that is a very common thing to happen as well, for one of the few things that seem to be generally agreed about the 'cause' of AS is that there is a genetic link. But the diagnosis was very helpful in a couple of ways. It let me understand Kenneth much better than I could have if I had been very different from him. And the more I was able to understand and help him, the more I was able to understand and help myself.

COMMON FEATURE 5: 'CRAZY' DECISIONS

People with AS often say that looking back, they don't understand how they made some of the crazy decisions they did – crazy, that is, in the sense of being the opposite of 'street-wise' and sometimes self-destructive. The kind of crazy decisions that hidden Aspies make are often about really important things – for example money, career and relationships.

In my case, for example, by the time I got my diagnosis I had been though three divorces. And I had forced myself through a law degree, even though I hated it from day one. As well as making crazy decisions, I didn't seem to have much common sense about how long it was sensible to stick at things for, and when would be a good time to change direction. Even though I only ever worked at it part-time, I stuck at a career as a lawyer for 18 years. It is hard to understand why, because I knew it was all wrong for me from the beginning.

COMMON FEATURE 6: BACKGROUND FEELINGS

Overall I always had a background feeling that I was just about coping; that life was a terrible effort; and that there was something about me that I was hiding from people – something that was somehow 'wrong'. I struggled with depression a lot, and at those times much of what I was putting my time and energy into seemed pointless. Even though I had a so-called successful career in law, for example, it never felt worthwhile. Again, these kinds of feelings are commonly reported among Aspies who go for adult diagnosis.

I didn't want to admit it for a long time, but I was being completely untrue to myself. It was as if the 'real me' had gone to sleep, and I had been taken over by an actor who played a role. I think that was the real root of my depression. There was a conflict that went on inside me for years. Part of me would have preferred to stay asleep. Another part of me wouldn't let it happen.

For most of my adult life, I used to have a recurrent night terror. It was so horrible the only word I could use to describe it properly is 'hellish'. Usually I couldn't remember much detail about it, but it always ended up the same way. I knew I was sleeping and that I needed to waken up. If I didn't waken, the real me was going to die. I would struggle with every bit of my strength to waken up, terrified I wouldn't be able to. The panic and terror that gripped me was extreme. During those moments I knew the 'real me' had been lost somewhere along the way and I had no idea who I was looking for or how to find her.

COMMON FEATURE 7: WEARING A MASK AND/OR LEARNING TO FIT IN

I have always been pretty determined and I am inclined to analyse things a lot; that part of me has been very useful over the years. I have used it to help me find out how most things work, so to speak. Overall I think I usually have a good idea of what it is that people expect of me. But trying to work out things like that can be a very tiring process, and it can use up an awful lot of energy. Maybe that is part of the reason why I made so many crazy decisions throughout my life – especially in terms of relationships and career.

My true identity lay far behind my mask and it was a slow process for me to find myself again. I went to counselling to try and get to the root of my problems and ended up staying there for about 17 years. I made a lot of progress through that, and faced some real inner demons. When I finally got the diagnosis of AS, it was a real breakthrough in the long journey of accepting and forgiving myself.

Why did I eventually decide to go for a diagnosis? In the end I decided that life was too short and I didn't want to go to my grave without ever having discovered who I really was. Also I got too worn out to keep up a pretence any more, which was just as well, because the price I was paying was higher than I realised.

COMMON FEATURE 8: COMING TO TERMS AND ACCEPTANCE

I know that all must sound pretty dark and depressing, but it is a part of the big picture and so it needs to be confronted. Wearing a mask always takes its toll in the end in one way or another. Life as a hidden Aspie can be tough.

But there is the good news as well. Getting a diagnosis is one of the best decisions I have ever made. I can say that now, two years on, for the changes did not happen overnight. It took time, but gradually I began to feel better about myself. I no longer have the night terrors that I used to have, and I think that in itself says a lot! A lot of the need to pretend that I used to have has lifted from me now, and there is something very liberating about that.

Maybe you could say it's a pity I didn't manage to own my AS and be true to myself earlier in my life, but on the other hand, 'better late than never'! Everything in life has its own right timing, and the diagnosis put me on a path I needed to find. Many things in my life have changed for the better in the last two years since I got my diagnosis. I will tell you more about that in Chapter 12. But before that let's go back to Asperger Syndrome and its relationships with both autism and giftedness.

Chapter 9

ASPERGERS AND AUTISM?

If you want to try and understand AS, there are plenty of official definitions available. Take this one for example:

> *Asperger Syndome is a form of autism. It is a lifelong disability that affects how a person makes sense of the world, processes information and relates to other people.*
> *National Autistic Society 2008*

But there are very few things about Asperger Syndrome that are entirely straightforward, and even this basic definition is subject to controversy. The controversy is centred mainly on two issues:

1. whether AS really is a form of autism; and

2. whether it is right to call it a disability.

In some circles it is regarded as inaccurate, misleading and even offensive to say that AS is 'a form of autism'. The people who object to this, understandably, tend to be people who have been diagnosed with AS but are at the top end of the spectrum (ability-wise). They may realise they are intelligent – sometimes exceptionally so. They may be gifted in some areas, academically or creatively. And they may be very 'successful' in the eyes of the world. But in terms of fitting into the world, they recognise that they are something of a misfit.

On the other hand they do not like to think of themselves as autistic, and often they feel very strongly and passionately about this. Interestingly, they are not alone. There are some professionals and academics who also unofficially disagree with the idea of classifying Asperger Syndrome as a form of autism.

Is AS really a form of autism? It is an important question – partly because looking into it can help us understand Asperger Syndrome, and partly because when AS is portrayed as a form of autism, that is bound to put people at the top end of the spectrum (ability-wise) off coming forward for assessment. It makes little sense to them to think of themselves as having any form of autism, and it is also very unappealing for them to think of themselves in this way.

PICTURES OF AUTISM

If you think of autism for a moment, what picture comes into your head?

Impressions of autism are changing all the time, but even these days when people think of autism, the picture they have in their head is likely to be of a particular stereotype. They may picture, for example, a child sitting in the corner rocking and withdrawn, and they may associate autism with mental disability or retardation. But most people who are diagnosed with AS do not fit that picture at all.

ALTERNATIVE ANGLES ON AS

So is Asperger Syndrome a form of high functioning autism, or is it a separate condition in its own right?

One school of thought sees Asperger Syndrome as a sort of subset of autism, a bit more like a distant cousin. Some people see it as a distinct condition albeit with similar features, and say that it should have a category of its own.

Rather than see AS as a disability, some people prefer to see it as a different way of being or personality type. Just as the Asperger spectrum is sometimes seen as a big umbrella or spectrum in itself, it can also be seen as part of the larger autistic spectrum. And the autistic spectrum can be seen as part of an even bigger spectrum, which is the spectrum of humanity with all its range and diversity. And sometimes that's not a bad way to look at things – for everyone, as they say, has a little bit of autism in them – and often that is where the most interesting parts of our personality lie!

Another helpful way of understanding AS is to see it as a developmental disorder as opposed to a disability. Aspies do generally develop at different rates to most other people.

People say AS is a 'lifelong' condition and in a sense that is true, because your basic personality doesn't change, but with determination there is a lot you can do to change aspects of yourself – if you really want to, that is.

COMPARING AUTISM AND AS

The main thing is this. It is generally agreed that there is a link of some sort between autism and Asperger Syndrome. So whatever view you take, if you want to understand Asperger Syndrome, it is bound to be useful to take a quick look at some of the core issues surrounding autism.

The impairments that lie at the core of autism are to be found mainly in the areas of communicating, relating and processing information. These areas are affected in the person with AS as well, but sometimes quite differently and usually less obviously.

People with both autism and AS are usually somewhat removed from the world, but again there are differences. If you think of it this way it can be helpful. People with autism tend to live in a world of their own, whereas people with Asperger Syndrome tend to live in this world, but on their terms.

Both autism and AS are officially regarded as disabilities, but unlike AS there is generally no controversy about autism being classed as a disability. When someone is physically disabled, that it is easy to see and understand. But even with other disabilities which are not physical, it is usually quite easy to spot where the disability or impairment lies – whether for example it is in the area of mental illness, retardation or functioning.

When my son was first diagnosed, I was given a little AS information card, which is about the size of a business card and designed to sum up the condition to people who know nothing about it. It gave an explanation of Asperger Syndrome which included the following:

> People with Asperger Syndrome can come across as eccentric, rude, arrogant and gauche. Please be patient. They do not mean to offend.

This is an interesting description because it clearly identifies what may well be the first impression that a stranger will have of a person with AS – not that he has a 'disability' but that he is 'eccentric, rude, arrogant or gauche'.

If someone comes across like that, other people are likely to just find them off-putting, and they will find it hard to see them as having a disability. It can be very hard to explain to an outsider who has never heard of AS where the disability lies. If you have ever tried, I'm sure you know what I mean.

A 'RELATIONSHIP DISABILITY'?

Even if we accept that Asperger Syndrome can, from any point of view, properly be described as a disability – what area of life does it affect most? The official definition said that AS 'affects how a person…relates to other people'; when you view it from this angle it can provide some helpful insights.

Aspies can come across as intelligent and articulate, but they are poor at non-verbal communication, and this can have a massive impact on how they relate to others and how others perceive them.

A good way to understand AS therefore is to see it as a 'relationship disability' in that Aspies are generally said to be poor at 'social skills'. But what do we really mean when we talk about social skills? Are they really that important? And if part of the disability of AS is in the area of social skills, is that really such a big deal?

When we talk about social skills, what we are really talking about are the skills that we use when we relate to other people – whether it be our loved ones, our teachers or employers, our friends or colleagues, or strangers that we meet on the street. Maybe if you have never thought about it before, they doesn't sound like much, but social skills are actually extremely important.

Everyone has problems with social skills from time to time, to some extent or other. The difference for a person with Asperger Syndrome is that the difficulties can be extreme, and they can have a major impact on his life.

BEING SOCIALLY GIFTED

Sometimes to help us to understand something, it can be useful to look at its opposite. So let's think of it this way. Bring into your mind someone you know whom you would regard as being the polar opposite of a person with Asperger Syndrome. Or if you can't think of someone, imagine a stereotype of a person who is very socially successful – the kind of person that I think of as socially gifted as opposed to socially handicapped – and analyse what it is about that person that makes him or her 'successful'. We have all come across people like this.

Socially gifted people will be adept at some of the higher-level social skills. Here is a list of some of their attributes, and the things they will probably be good at. They are likely to:

- enjoy socialisation and being with people

- be good at knowing what is expected in company

- understand social rules well

- be good team players

- be considered to be pleasant, friendly charismatic and 'charming'

- be tactful and diplomatic

- have natural empathy

- be skilful at anticipating and meeting the expectations of others

- be naturally sensitive to the feelings of others

- be generally good at 'playing the game'.

These are the people who are popular and successful, and they generally have a much easier ride through life than Aspies. They are easier to get on with and they do not challenge us in the same way as an Aspie might. But that does not necessarily mean they are in any way better people. It is interesting to consider this: a person who is socially gifted may also be good at 'lying well', at least in the sense of telling small white lies easily and convincingly, and 'being economical with the truth'.

THE IMPACT OF A RELATIONSHIP DISABILITY?

In comparison to the socially gifted person, the typical Aspie is light years away. He lacks social skills which are much more basic than those on the above list, so it doesn't really do Asperger Syndrome justice to think of it only in terms of a disability which 'affects social skills'.

If you are not familiar with the term 'social skills' (as it is used within the autism world), then it can sound like it is referring to higher-level social skills such as charm and charisma. If you had this impression, then being poor at social skills might not seem like such a big deal.

Maybe rather than thinking of it as a disability affecting social skills, it would be more meaningful to think of it as a relationship disability.

IN SUMMARY

It would be hard to overstate the importance of relationships in the life of the human being. Even though we can all get caught up from time to time in the hurly burly of life, we know this in our heart. When something big or traumatic happens in our lives, it can often trigger us to reconsider our values. At times like this we can see very clearly what does and what doesn't matter to us. We realise that a lot of what we spend our time and energy on is of little or no importance in the bigger picture.

Earlier in this chapter we asked whether a disability affecting social skills was really such a big deal. We need to realise that it is, for the quality of our relationships is the measure of the quality of our lives. Autism affects how people relate to the world in a fairly obvious way, in that people with autism are usually quite clearly withdrawn from the world and they are likely to have difficulties with verbal and non-verbal communication. Asperger Syndrome also affects the way a person relates to the world, but even though the effect may be much more subtle, it is still very real.

Chapter 10

ASPERGERS AND GIFTEDNESS?

People on the autistic spectrum are sometimes remarkably gifted, original and creative. Let's take a few famous modern-day examples.

- Stephen Wiltshire's remarkable ability to draw from memory with uncanny accuracy has astounded people to such an extent that several documentaries have been made about him.

- Temple Grandin has used her exceptional ability to think visually to come up with innovative designs for humane livestock facilities.

- Daniel Tammett has also baffled the experts because of his astounding brain. He is conversant in eleven languages and holds the European record for reciting pi (π) to 22,514 digits (in five hours and nine minutes).

These may seem to be fascinating examples of a rare phenomenon, but there are certainly reasons to believe that the connection between AS and giftedness is closer than is generally believed. Here are some of them:

1. Ability can be hard to measure and detect in Aspies.

2. There tend to be certain similarities between gifted people and Aspies (in terms of how they think, and the difficulties they encounter).

3.   Many exceptionally gifted people show traits of AS.

1. ABILITY CAN BE HARD TO MEASURE AND DETECT IN ASPIES

How do we form an impression of or measure ability in anyone? Usually it is by observation and testing. But observation and testing can be misleading for assessing the true ability of a person with AS, for various reasons: (1) he may have a jagged profile of ability; (2) his development pattern may be unusual; (3) he may have unusual and all-absorbing interests, and not be interested in the things he is expected to be interested in; (4) he is likely to under-perform.

It is interesting to note that all four of these reasons often apply to people who are exceptionally gifted as well.

Jagged profile

It is common for a child with AS to have a 'jagged profile' meaning that his ability level is well above average in some areas and well below average in others. This makes it hard for an accurate assessment to be made of his ability.

Development

A child will normally be viewed as 'bright' if he passes developmental milestones either on time or earlier than expected. However, because AS is a developmental disability, it is quite common for him to be behind in certain areas (though he may simultaneously be well advanced in certain others).

Disinterest

It can be very hard to motivate an AS child to do what he does not want to do or does not see the point of. As well as that, he may be interested in obscure areas that are of little interest to anyone else.

If he is not interested in something (some aspect of his school work for example), there is a good chance that he will not even try to apply himself, and that makes it impossible to assess accurately what he would be capable of if he was interested and he did apply himself.

For the same reason, even if something like a standard IQ test is used to test the ability of someone with AS, the result can be misleading. If he is not interested in the test, or does not apply himself to it, then the test result may be lower than he would otherwise be capable of. For this reason a high IQ score can be taken as 'proof' of high ability, whereas a low IQ score may not necessarily be 'proof' of low ability.

Under-performance

Generally speaking, the education system and in particular the exam system does not suit people with Asperger Syndrome well, so there is a good chance that they will under-perform academically. If they do stand out at school in any way, the reason is more likely to be that they are causing problems because of behaviour issues or failure to comply. But often people who turn out to be remarkable, original and gifted as adults have been at best mediocre at school.

As adults Aspies are more likely than the average person to end up with a job for which they are 'overqualified' (in terms of ability), or even with no job at all. Somehow the system is stacked against them. Obviously there is little direct connection between Asperger Syndrome and 'doing well' in the world.

Another difficulty is that the Aspie is unlikely to dance to someone else's tune or jump through hoops that are of no interest to him, and may not be good at functioning in the world.

FOR EXAMPLE
In the film 'Rainman', Dustin Hoffman played a character who presented a particularly intriguing image of Asperger Syndrome. He had a lot of obvious difficulties and could barely function in the 'normal' world, but he was exceptionally gifted with numbers. The character was based on Kim Peake, who has in reality one of the most amazing brains in the world, astounding everyone by his ability to memorise and calculate enormous numbers more quickly than a computer.

2. SIMILARITIES BETWEEN ASPIES AND GIFTED PEOPLE

People with Asperger Syndrome have brains that work differently from the brains of most other people. They tend to be obsessive and have a great capacity for absorbing and retaining information when it is on a topic that appeals to them. And when they are particularly interested in something, they can gather and catalogue quite phenomenal levels of factual information. We see similar tendencies in people who are recognised to be gifted.

The experience of NAGC (National Association for Gifted Children) tends to support the idea that there is some kind of link between giftedness and Aspergers type difficulties. Just as in the case of children with AS, a high proportion of children who are academically gifted also have a difficult and unhappy time – both at school and socially. Many of their difficulties are similar to those that the diagnosed Aspie will experience – social difficulties, boredom, poor motivation, not seeing the point, behaviour problems etc.

Interestingly, when a child is gifted in any area other than academic, problems like these seem to be much less likely. Academically gifted children and AS children seem to have a lot in common. Both can come across as arrogant and awkward for example, and both can be a real challenge to parents and teachers. But if a child is gifted in something other than the academic, this tends to be viewed and treated differently. A special interest or talent in some area of sport, art or music for example is more socially acceptable and is more likely to be nurtured and encouraged.

3. EXCEPTIONALLY GIFTED PEOPLE AND ASPIES – SIMILAR PROFILES

Obviously there are highly gifted and remarkable people in the world today, but it is hard to say how many of them fit the typical AS profile. It would be interesting to do some kind of analysis in order to find out, but it would be difficult to get the information that would be needed. And it would be a risky business to speculate about people who are still alive, because whether they have AS or not is really their own business. There is a lot of speculation being done, however (which is freely available on the web naturally enough). But from a legal point of view it is safer to analyse people who are dead! That is why researchers who are looking into the link between Asperger Syndrome and giftedness tend to focus on historical figures.

Historical figures are often so well known that there is plenty of information available about them upon which research can be based. They have usually had volumes written about their life and personalities by way of biographies and analyses from various different points of view. Academic researchers who are interested in the link between AS and giftedness have been able to make use of materials like these to do some deep and detailed studies, which have given us some remarkable insights.

Recent research has shown that many truly remarkable and gifted people throughout history have had profiles which suggest that they did indeed have Asperger Syndrome. The following is a thumb-nail sketch of a selection of these people:

- **Hans Christian Anderson** had a very difficult and unhappy time at school. He seems generally to have been a misfit, found it hard to relate to other people socially, was prone to depression and wrote compulsively. He had great problems with grammar and spelling, and was told by the headmaster that he was stupid and would never amount to anything.

- **Lewis Carroll** found it hard to fit in socially and to engage in small talk. It seemed to be easier for him to relate to children than adults. He was intensely interested in trains and also in collecting and inventing puzzles, stories and nonsense verse; he was also a compulsive letter writer. In later years he kept a register of his letters, which showed that over a 35-year period he wrote and received 98,721 letters.

- **Albert Einstein** was an unusual and withdrawn child. He was a late talker, but showed an early interest in maths and physics. At school he was well behaved but dreamy, but he did tend to ignore authority. He did not perform at all well, and his teachers considered him to be mentally slow, dreamy and unsociable. Throughout his life he was isolated and socially awkward. Like Temple Grandin, he was very much a visual thinker.

- **Beethoven** did badly at school and showed no early sign whatsoever of his musical genius. He was solitary and controlling, and often behaved in socially inappropriate ways. He was very prone to depression, but was obsessed by music, which seems to have been his anti-depressant.

- **WB Yeats** was shy and eccentric, even as a child. He did not do well in school and was bullied. Like Hans Christian Anderson, he was told that he would never amount to anything by his headmaster. He had obsessive interests, for example in some forms of Irish folklore, and often displayed socially inappropriate behaviour. Sometimes, for example, he walked round the streets of Dublin flapping his arms while he recited and composed poetry.

- **Michaelangelo** was a shy, introspective child and a solitary adult. His conversational skills were poor and other people tended to find him unapproachable. His domestic habits were said to be squalid, and he struggled with depression. He often became so intensively absorbed in his work that he forgot to eat or sleep.

- **Wolfgang Amadeus Mozart**, despite being a musical genius, found it hard to relate to the world and to find his place in it. From a very early age he was a dreamer and obsessed by music. He was very aware of his giftedness, but even though he composed about 600 works in his short life (35 years) he never found financial security. This was at least in part because he did not know how to behave towards people with power and influence who could have helped his career.

- **Vincent Van Gogh** felt like an outsider all his life and found it very hard to get on with other people. He too often behaved in socially inappropriate ways and quarrelled a lot with other people. He was seen as eccentric and a recluse, but took solace from his painting, which he was very obsessive about.

- **Andy Warhol** was an exceptionally shy child who showed an early obsession with painting. He was isolated and withdrawn, and his reading and spelling skills were very poor. Even as an adult, when he was in company he would draw compulsively, while other people talked round him. He had a strange way of talking to other people, sometimes just using single words to communicate his ideas.

WHAT DOES ALL THIS MEAN?

When an individual displays both giftedness and AS, it may mean one of many things. It may mean, for example, that:

- he simply happens to have both conditions as two separate entities which have no relationship to each other. In other words it is nothing more than a coincidence, or

- his giftedness is an intrinsic part of his Asperger Syndrome. If that were true, it might suggest that more Aspies have elements of giftedness than we generally imagine, or

- his Asperger Syndrome is an intrinsic part of his giftedness. If that were true, it might suggest that more gifted people have AS than we generally imagine.

The nature of the link may be mysterious, but there certainly seems to be an overlap. The connection is probably best understood by visualising AS and giftedness as two intersecting circles. One circle represents AS and the other giftedness. They are not the same thing, but they do overlap. The intersection represents people who are both gifted and Aspie, but there are also gifted people who do not have AS, just as there are Aspies who are not gifted.

It is hard to know the extent of the overlap. It may seem to be something like this:

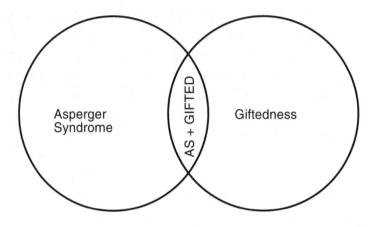

Figure 10.1 Apparent overlap between AS and giftedness

But if we include hidden Aspies who are gifted, it may look more like this.

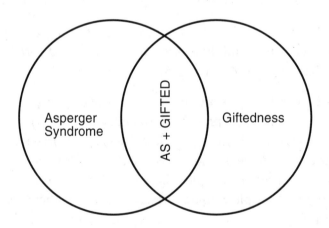

Figure 10.2 The overlap if hidden (gifted) Aspies are also included

And if we include Aspies who appear not to be gifted, but whose gifts are so far undiscovered, it may look more like this.

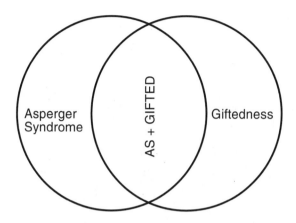

Figure 10.3 The overlap if diagnosed Aspies with undiscovered gifts are included

It is interesting to think that there may well be a lot of hidden Aspies in the world, and that they are likely to be at the highly able or even gifted end of the AS spectrum. In the next chapter we will look at how we might identify such hidden Aspies!

Chapter 11

IDENTIFYING HIDDEN ASPIES

Just to recap, there are reasons to believe that there are many 'hidden Aspies' in the world today – people, that is, who either have Asperger Syndrome but have not been diagnosed, or people who have been diagnosed but are keeping the fact private. Part of the reason for this must be lack of awareness; part of it must be the fact that AS does not have a particularly good 'image'.

It is hard to get to the bottom of the complex relationship between AS and giftedness, but it does seem likely that there are more gifted people than we realise who have undiagnosed AS (or who at least have AS traits). It is also reasonable to assume that there are more Aspies than we realise who have unrecognised gifts.

I wonder if anyone you know is a hidden Aspie. Or maybe even you are a hidden Aspie yourself? Most people have at least some AS traits that they keep hidden – from themselves sometimes as well as from the rest of the world.

But how do Aspies stay hidden?

WEARING MASKS

Often, hidden Aspies wear a mask to hide who they are. They may do that in order to get by, to feel that they fit in, and also to fool others that they fit in. It is a real pity that people feel they have to hide who they really are. If you feel the need to do that, it must mean that to some extent you do not feel good enough about who you really are. But being untrue to yourself is never a good idea. It is a loss to yourself and to the world. You will probably end up unhappy and fail to fulfil your true potential.

It is hard to work out why some some Aspies wear masks and some don't. I have seen both, for I spent years wearing a mask myself, but my son Kenneth is the opposite, for he has never worn a mask. His Aspie-ness is out there for all to see and there is no pretence. As far as I can tell, he never does a thing in order to fit in just for the sake of fitting in, just as he never does a thing to please solely in order to keep on the right side of people.

From time to time the two of us have discussed this, and his view is that he had absolutely no choice. Wearing a mask would never have even been an option for him, and it would never have even entered his head to be any way other than true to himself.

That kind of attitude does not make for an easy path through life – for him I mean. And it also makes it difficult for the people around him (especially the ones in authority). But despite all that, there is something very refreshing and admirable about his attitude that I have never been able to deny. And for showing me in such a graphic way that it really is possible to live life completely true to yourself, I will always owe him a huge debt of gratitude.

GOOD ACTORS

Another thing that hidden Aspies have in common is that they know how to 'act the part'. I have heard this said time and time again by people who have been diagnosed as adults, and I can see looking back that it is true for me too. Aspies can be very skilful actors; their difficulties and Aspie traits can be so subtle that they are hard to spot unless you are an expert. Sometimes hidden Aspies do such a good job that they honestly end up fooling themselves – most of the time anyway.

Somewhere along the way, I suppose I must have learned to act, but I can't remember any time when I made a specific decision to do so. I think I can perform a role very convincingly when I am in a social setting, but it can be very tiring, and I don't like to do it for too long without taking a break.

There is a common experience among people with Asperger Syndrome as well, in particular people who come across well socially; the jargon is that they 'present well'. But 'presenting well' can take more out of them than people would ever guess. I have talked to Aspies who say they go to bed every night completely exhausted from the strain of their 'performance' socially.

The acting that hidden Aspies do when they perform socially is something very different from stage drama, because with stage drama you know you are taking on a role that is not your own. It is only for a specific amount of time and you are aware that you are acting, because you have deliberately and consciously chosen to. That means you don't confuse the role with who you really are. Acting a part in life rather than on stage is a bit more sinister, because you can end up not knowing who you are, and if you do this over many years, it is a hard place to come back from.

If there is some link between AS and giftedness, then it would be a good idea to try and create a more Asperger-friendly climate in the world – one which would be more positive and encouraging to Aspies. But even if there were no link whatsoever, it would still be important.

LOOKING FOR CLUES

At the end of the day, only a qualified diagnostician can properly assess an individual so as to tell for certain whether he has AS or not, but it can be interesting to consider how we might be able to identify hidden Aspies. What clues can we look out for? What are the typical characteristics of hidden Aspies?

Gender

At the moment the rate of diagnosis for males as against females is about 8:1. Does that really mean there are actually very few females with AS? Maybe so. Or maybe it means that they are just not being picked up for diagnosis as easily as males. The first and most obvious factor that I believe allowed me to stay hidden for so long is simply the fact that I am female. I wonder how many other females are going through life the way I did.

Females tend to be more malleable and they are also naturally more skilful at tuning in to the expectations of others. I know this is a generalisation, but like most generalisations there is truth in it. Females can get on particularly well in life if they become well behaved, compliant and pleasing, and if they fulfil the roles expected of them as they go through the various stages of life (infant, child, school girl, student, wife, mother, employee etc.).

It would not be surprising if undiagnosed females are more common than you would think. It would certainly help explain why the number of females being diagnosed is so much lower than the number of males.

Personality

Aspies who are extremely compliant are more likely to stay hidden. Instead of projecting their problems outside themselves, they hold onto them and keep them deeply and secretly tucked away inside. This can be a problem for them, because they are less likely to get the attention and help they need – children who don't cause problems at school have less chance of being picked up and diagnosed.

But it can be a bit more complex than that, for sometimes people who do well at hiding their Aspie-ness can be very compliant in some ways and yet very rebellious and single-minded in others. And as we saw earlier, an important key to understanding AS is that it is a condition of extremes.

You can sometimes see both of two opposite extremes in people with AS. As a young child, for example, most of the time I was extremely compliant and pleasing – in fact I would say that I was probably as extreme in being compliant as my son was the opposite! But there was another side to me as well that was the exact opposite.

When we are children we all develop our own strategies to help us deal with the world, and what these are largely depends on our personality. I was a quiet and vigilant child and I put huge amounts of effort into trying to get things right, working out what seemed to be expected of me and then delivering it. It was an unnatural way to operate, but it became second nature for me. Aspies with this kind of personality are more likely to stay hidden.

The age factor

Because awareness of AS is so widespread today, it can be hard to remember that not so long ago conditions such as Asperger Syndrome were not recognised in schools. The approach to children with complex difficulties even as recently as a generation or two ago was much less enlightened. So another factor that makes it more likely for people to go undiagnosed is their age. Hidden Aspies are likely to be older – the most common stage of life for people to get diagnosed is during the school years.

I know quite a few people who were diagnosed as adults and who had extreme difficulties at school. Some were extreme enough to end up expelled or sent to special schools or behavioural units. If they were school age today, there is a good chance that they would be diagnosed and receive the support they would have needed – but the situation used to be very different.

Gifted and successful

Aspies can be very focused and obsessive, and they can end up becoming very successful when their focus and obsession happens to be on something which the world sees as valuable. They can become very successful academically, for example. I have heard Tony Attwood refer to universities as 'sheltered workshops for people with Asperger Syndrome'.

A lot of very intelligent and academically gifted hidden Aspies must find universities to be a comfortable environment. But I imagine there are a lot of very gifted and successful people in business or in the arts as well who are hidden.

Success and high achievement can sometimes serve to mask difficulties that an individual is coping with in private – social and emotional difficulties for example. And it may not occur either to the individual or to the people around him to look into the possibility that he may have AS.

Asperger Syndrome in the family

It is not uncommon for people in a similar position as me to go for diagnosis – someone in the family circle has been diagnosed; they have got to know what AS is; they recognise the traits in themselves. It is widely accepted that AS has a genetic link. So where there is one diagnosis in the family, it is not unreasonable to expect that there may be other people in the family who at least have similar traits.

AS personality traits

Ironically enough, some of the typical traits of AS are also factors that allow Aspies to stay hidden – for example the typical AS determination may allow a person to work very hard to fit in, and to overcome difficulties. When hidden Aspies are determined enough, they can 'overcome' a lot of the difficulties of AS so well that it can be hard for people to tell they ever had that difficulty, or even that they have AS.

Other clues

It is worth noting that hidden Aspies sometimes stay hidden in other more unfortunate ways. For example they can be misdiagnosed with some kind of mental illness. Or they can slip through the cracks and turn to drugs or alcohol.

Chapter 12

HAPPY ENDING, HAPPY BEGINNING

There are three things that I would love this book to accomplish. The first is that I would love people to see AS in a more positive light. The second is related to the first – I would love people to understand AS better; not only AS as it is in people who are officially diagnosed with AS, but even the AS traits in the people around them, and in themselves. The third is that I would love more people – and in particular more females – to come forward for diagnosis and to open up about their own AS.

I think in order to accomplish these things, I will need to tell you a bit more about my own story and what I have learned from it. So this chapter contains an account of how AS has affected me and how I have related to it.

CLICHÉS

It is easy for me to understand why people go for years without knowing or even wanting to consider the possibility that they might have AS, because I have been there myself. But I am glad I did not stay there! It still seems strange to me that I spent so many years in denial. But I suppose everything has its proper timing in life, and the time was not right until a few years ago.

The bottom line is this – life has improved quite radically since I got my diagnosis, so that today I can finally say that I am glad I have Asperger

Syndrome. Or maybe it's more accurate to say I am very glad I now realise and accept the fact that I have Asperger Syndrome. I am not saying that for everyone who gets an adult diagnosis like me, life will change; even if changes do happen in your life, they might happen slowly.

Things did not change overnight for me, but there was something about getting the diagnosis that put me on the path I needed to be on. Maybe it was because I was finally starting to be honest with myself, but it helped me in a way that nothing else could.

GUILT

Probably the main thing the diagnosis did for me was to lift a lot of the guilt I had been constantly carrying round. I felt guilty about so many things. The main one was probably the mess I always seemed to make of relationships, but there didn't need to be a specific reason. I just had a background feeling of guilt and unworthiness most of the time no matter what. It was just a vague sense that I didn't quite fit and that I wasn't getting things quite right. And that is a common feeling among hidden Aspies.

Before I had my diagnosis, I was the same person obviously, but I was trying to be someone else. It has been a long hard route, but today I embrace my Asperger Syndrome. I could explain it by using some well-worn phrases. I could say for example that since my diagnosis I have started to discover who it is that I really am. Or that I have reclaimed parts of myself that had been cut off for years. Or that I had been hiding behind a mask and I needed to remove it. Or that since my diagnosis, at last I have begun to understand freedom. Or that at this stage of my life I am becoming more true to myself than I have ever been before. Those things probably all sound like clichés – but they are all true in a way!

One of the ways in which I used to get through life was to work out what other people seemed to expect from me and then to try and deliver it. In retrospect this seems like a crazy way to live, and when I think about it now it seems so false that I cringe. But I had been doing it for so long I didn't even know I was doing it. It had become second nature to me to wear a mask.

As time went by and I got older I noticed I was getting more and more tired of it. I had always been prone to depression, but it was getting worse and also more frequent. I was given time off work and seemed to need more and more periods of isolation. During these times I would lock myself in my house and lie down for days.

When I went through one of these periods, the only thing I felt motivated to go out for was chocolate. I put on about two and a half stone from binge eating. Of course that only made me feel worse!

CHOICES

I was kind of aware that I had made some choices in my life that seemed crazy, and that I was still paying the price for some of them. My career was a good example of this.

Before I left school I had been very interested in creative things. I loved calligraphy, drawing and writing poetry and above all I loved music. I had enjoyed playing the piano for years and I had taught myself a bit of guitar. I wasn't great at it, but I used to play around on the guitar and I wrote some songs for my own amusement. I didn't think about the future much at that age, and I didn't know what I wanted to do with myself by way of a career, but it never really occurred to me that it would be anything other than something creative.

I suppose I must have applied to get into the law faculty at Queens University, but I really don't remember doing it. I certainly don't know why I would have been interested in it. It was obvious I was wrong for it. Most things felt false to me, but song writing was one of the few things that seemed real. It opened up a whole new world and I can't think of anything that I found more satisfying at the time. For a very short period I became passionate about all these creative things, especially the song writing.

When my A level results came through I didn't think about my decision very much. It seemed like quite a prize to have done well enough to be offered a place in the law faculty. I knew other people who hadn't made it, and that made it seem like more of an achievement. My parents were clearly delighted, so I accepted the place.

I went along with the idea largely because it seemed to be what was expected of me. It seems crazy now, but even though it was a very big decision, it didn't seriously occur to me to make it on any other basis. A life-changing decision like a career should not be made solely on the basis of what other people expect, but I think in retrospect that I was used to making decisions on that basis.

It is hard to imagine a degree that was less well suited to my personality and interests, and that made it very hard work. But I struggled on through, managed to get my law degree, and ended up working as a solicitor for 18 years.

As a lawyer I felt like a complete misfit most of the time, so it is hard to understand how I stuck it for so long. The only way I can explain it is that the feeling of being a misfit was something familiar to me, so I didn't know any different. If I hadn't had AS, I probably would have known in the first place that it was a job that I was completely unsuited for.

But as well as that, there is something about Asperger Syndrome that can make the process of decision-making far from straightforward. And it also makes it very hard to change direction, so that even when you find yourself in a situation that you hate, you feel you have to leave things as they are. You tell yourself it's OK rather than face the prospect of making changes.

Those things added together meant I ended up stuck in a demanding career that I hated for about 18 years. In the end I never managed to work at it full time, but I learned to do what was expected of me and functioned as a reasonably successful lawyer. The price was high though. It is very tiring to do something you are not meant to do for years. In the intervening years I was married three times and had two children, and my children and law career took up most of my energy.

But by the time I was diagnosed I had already given up law, mostly because when Kenneth was younger it became impossible to run a law practice and also to do everything that was needed to look after his interests. I tried getting involved in a few other, less demanding jobs instead, including working for the National Autistic Society. Then when I got my diagnosis, I resolved never again to be untrue to myself and it began to occur to me that what I really needed to do was to try and rediscover my creativity.

FINDING MY MUSIC AGAIN

Seventeen years in therapy had given me a lot of answers. It had helped me understand a lot about myself, human nature, relationships, and what makes people tick. So it was a great help, but I often felt I was going through the motions, and that there was some kind of missing link. The missing link turned out to be Asperger Syndrome, and the diagnosis allowed me to find it.

My life is completely different now from what it used to be. I suppose I am finally doing the kind of things I should have been doing all along, and they are all creative things. The book *Asperger Syndrome, the Swan and the Burglar* was the first time I ever wrote a story that was purely imaginative and creative. It was influenced by my experience of AS of course, but it came from my heart and not my head. Then I started painting, purely for relaxation and found I loved it. And I began to look around for a way in which I could get back into the world of music.

As I said, the AS diagnosis opened up some interesting doors for me. One of these doors opened about a year ago when I met singer-songwriter Bap Kennedy (www.bapkennedy.com). He first came into my life when he started teaching my son, Kenneth, to play the guitar. It was soon clear to me that as well as being a gifted musician he had another very special gift. There was something about him and the way he dealt with children with Asperger Syndrome that helped them relax and get in touch with their own musical creativity. I heard the same thing from the Mums of other children he was working with as well. Bap was working wonders and bringing a little magic into the lives of children with autism and Asperger Syndrome around Northern Ireland.

There was something in his manner that was very open. He was easy to trust, and before long I decided to take a risk and let him in on my secret! I told him about my diagnosis and the strange way I had resisted it for so long. And I also told him of my interest in music and the song writing, and how I had locked it away along with the Asperger part of me. Eventually I took a risk and let him hear some of the songs I had written, and he liked them enough to want to produce an album for me.

And when I think now about how much my music means to me, it seems hard to understand how I could have locked it away for so many years. The album feels like the most exciting, satisfying and worthwhile thing I have ever done.

I was lucky enough to meet a man who welcomed and encouraged the part of me that I had been running from for years. He helped me overcome many of my fears – fear of change, fear of revealing the hidden part of myself, fear of looking stupid, fear of failure and fear of the unknown. There was no judgement whatsoever in him, and that made all the difference.

None of it would have happened without him. But it would not have happened either if I had not gone down the route of claiming back the part of myself that had been locked away with my Asperger Syndrome. Over time he guided me to take risks and when I did I found out I was still OK. Without him my music would never have seen the light of day, because it was hidden away along with my Aspergers. And did he have a magic formula? Well, that could be another story!

THE LESSON?

When I blocked off the Asperger part of myself, I also blocked off the most creative and unique part of myself. To reclaim my music I needed to be true to myself. And part of that was owning my Asperger Syndrome.

And what lesson is there to be learned from all this? Maybe it's as simple as this – that above all we need to be true to ourselves. When we block off the parts of ourselves that make us uncomfortable, not only are we being untrue to who we really are, but we have no idea what else we are blocking off along with it.

Life is too short not to try and discover the whole truth about who you are – even if that does mean exploring the Asperger parts!

Chapter 13

THINKING POSITIVE!

We cannot control what we meet in life. We can only control how we see it and how we respond to it. One thing that can put us at an advantage is simply to see things differently – more positively that is. That is what the remaining sections of the book are about. They are probably more for dipping in to and referring to than reading from cover to cover.

This chapter contains the following:

1. Thinking of life as an RPG (role playing game) – and playing a positive game! This is mainly a discussion of how life can be made easier when you have a better understanding of the typical traits of Asperger Syndrome.

2. Appreciating appreciation. This contains an analysis of the concept of appreciation – what it really means and how we can go about appreciating Asperger Syndrome.

1. THINKING OF LIFE AS AN RPG – AND PLAYING A POSITIVE GAME!

My son really enjoys playing RPG's. Have you ever heard of them? RPG stands for 'role playing game'. I have never played, but apparently they are quite popular among some people with Asperger Syndrome. I was curious about why this might be, so I found out a bit about how they work.

I apologise in advance here to any RPG devotees (my son included!) for any errors in this description, but as far as I understand it, the basic principle of how RPG's work is as follows:

Each player assumes a role and each game is some kind of adventure into which an element of chance is introduced, usually by the throwing of dice. Players interact with each other strategically, but must keep within the rules of the game. The rules can be fairly complex, but they are clearly established. One person is nominated as Games Master (GM); players can refer to the GM if there is any need to clarify the rules.

As well as the rules of the game, each player must also keep within the limitations of his role. Each one has his own individual profile, which is made up of various factors – for example, he has certain skills, traits, attributes, powers, advantages, disadvantages and so on, and he can sometimes build up experience points (XP).

The rules of the game

Life is like an RPG in some ways – there are rules; people have roles; each of us has his own character; we all have certain advantages, disadvantages, skills, traits and so on. But there are differences as well. In real life there are a lot more rules, and it can be harder to find out what they are. The ones that are hardest of all to find out about are the social rules, i.e. the rules that govern how people relate to and behave towards each other.

To an Aspie it often seems as if everyone else knows what the social rules are, but they aren't written down anywhere and no one talks about them – except sometimes when they get broken. And there isn't a Games Master readily available who can easily clarify them for us.

For whatever reason, some people seem to find it easier than others to know the rules or to be able to find them out. In fact, most people do not think too much about the rules. It is almost as if they are born knowing them.

Real life is not a game of course, but just like an RPG, it can be 'played' in a smart and positive way. But it is very hard to keep the rules of a game when you don't know what they are. You can end up feeling as if you are hopeless at the game and get fed up playing. Other people can think you are hopeless as well. Or they might think you are breaking rules on purpose.

Any advantage you came into the game with may soon be eroded away, and you withdraw to the sidelines. This is one of the things that can happen when an Aspie does badly in the game of life by repeatedly breaking social rules.

> For people with AS, life can be a bit like playing an RPG without knowing the rules, and with no Games Master to refer to.

But there is a positive way of looking at all this.

If there are rules (as there are), then they are knowable, and people with AS can learn them. Realistically speaking, it will generally be a lot harder for them, and it will take a lot longer. Over time though, learning the rules can make life a lot easier.

An NT who is closely involved in the life of an Aspie can help in this learning process in important ways:

- He can ask himself what the rules are (because NT's often follow them without ever asking themselves this).

- He can explain rules very clearly to Aspies.

The person with AS needs to:

- accept that there are social rules that he is unaware of

- make up his mind to learn what they are

- remember to apply them and

- keep on learning and not give up.

This kind of approach can help improve communication between NT and Aspie and can remove a lot of the blame and frustration on both sides. Learning social rules can become a lifelong task for an Aspie, but if he can view it as a challenge he can apply himself to it in a determined way, and this can help make life easier for him.

Smart, positive play

Life is like an RPG in another way as well – each of us comes into it with different advantages and disadvantages. Obviously if you come into the game with advantages, you are off to a better start, but it does not guarantee you will do well, and vice versa. It is possible to lose advantages – and it is possible to gain them as well.

Life is like that too. We all have certain advantages and disadvantages, but we can 'play the game of life' wisely and strategically.

One thing that can put us at an advantage in life is when we know what it is reasonable to expect. No one likes the unpredictable, and this is even more true for people with AS. Life is easier when you have a better idea what to expect. What does that mean in reality? It means knowing yourself as well as you can, and it also means knowing what you are likely to come up against. That is why it can be so helpful for people with AS to get to know and understand as much as they can about AS. And that is why the A–Z of positives (p.152) contains a list of some of the issues and challenges that are likely to come up when you are dealing with Asperger Syndrome – along with some suggestions on how we can think positively about them! (See also Chapter 5, The Decoding Approach.)

2. APPRECIATING APPRECIATION

In order to be positive about anything, we need to appreciate it, but what does that really mean? The word 'appreciate' is a common enough word, and we all know what it means in an everyday kind of way. But it is worth taking a closer look at it, so we can see what it might mean in the context of Asperger Syndrome.

Defining appreciation

Wiktionary lists several slightly different meanings for the word 'appreciate', and they are all relevant in the context of Asperger Syndrome. They are:

- to be grateful or thankful

- to view as valuable

- to be aware of or to detect

- to increase in value

- to understand.

TO BE GRATEFUL OR THANKFUL

In the context of Asperger Syndrome what do we have to be grateful for? We all need to be grateful:

✓ for the gifts and contributions made both today and throughout history

✓ for the sheer effort it takes for Aspies to fit in and adapt as well as they do to a world that is not easy for them

✓ for the effort made by those who care for and take a positive interest in Asperger Syndrome.

TO VIEW AS VALUABLE

In the context of AS, we need to see the value in:

✓ each individual person who has been diagnosed with AS

✓ those qualities and traits that mark a person out so that he satisfies the criteria and

✓ the typical AS qualities in ourselves and each other – whether or not we have been diagnosed with AS.

TO BE AWARE OF OR TO DETECT

This meaning implies that we should be alert and vigilant about Asperger Syndrome – aware of what it is and what it is not. We should be able to recognise the traits and tendencies. That is very relevant in the context of AS, because the more we are aware of typical AS traits and tendencies, the better idea we will have of what it is reasonable to expect and what is 'normal'.

TO INCREASE IN VALUE

That is the meaning we use when we say, for example, that a piece of property has 'appreciated', when it has grown in value so as to become worth more money than it used to be. This meaning is in a way a natural by-product of the other meanings, because the more we appreciate AS in the other three senses, the more value we see in it.

TO UNDERSTAND

An important synonym which is listed for the word 'appreciate' is the word 'understand'. This is a less obvious meaning for 'appreciate', but it is actually very relevant in the context of AS. Why? Because understanding has to be our starting point and the basis of our appreciation. In a way all the other aspects of appreciation have to flow from understanding.

Chapter 14

POSITIVE PHILOSOPHIES

I am going to close this section of the book by offering a selection of positive points to ponder on various aspects of Asperger Syndrome.

ASPERGER SYNDROME AND SELF

Life is full of possibility and choice. There is so much for us to take an interest in – so many things we could learn about; so many different bases we could use to help us make our choices. Sometimes it is hard to know which of them to put our time and energy into.

'Know thyself' are words of advice that come to us from ancient wisdom.

Self-knowledge

When someone has AS, in a way that is nothing more than a label we put on him; and we need to be careful with labels. They can be very useful, but they are clumsy tools as well. The identity of a person is much greater and more complex than any label that we can put on him.

I wish they would only take me as I am.
Vincent Van Gogh

On the other hand, learning about AS offers great opportunity for self-knowledge, in the following ways:

- ✓ One of the key things about Asperger Syndrome is the word 'extreme' in that people with AS are 'like everyone else only more so'. In other words, Aspies present certain aspects of human nature in an extreme form – if people are honest with themselves, there is nothing about Asperger Syndrome, in its essence that they cannot identify with.

- ✓ As an extreme of human nature it allows all of us to find out more about human nature generally.

- ✓ Aspies have a better chance of understanding themselves and what makes them different from other people.

- ✓ It can help NT's learn more about themselves – in particular, the parts of themselves they might otherwise hide – from themselves as well as from the world.

- ✓ NT's have a better chance of understanding individual Aspies.

Remember everyone has some AS in them – and often the AS parts are really worth getting to know!

As we go through life, one of the things that can help us to find out who we are is when we have people around us who are similar to us – people who can understand and reflect who we are.

- ✓ When someone receives a diagnosis, he has a better chance of finding other people with AS whom he has a lot in common with and whom he can relate to.

✓ It is widely agreed that AS has strong genetic roots, so when one person in the family has been diagnosed, it may come to light that there is someone else in the family with AS, or at least with AS traits.

It is better to be a first rate version of yourself than a second rate version of somebody else.

Self-mastery and self-development

We all need to feel there are some things in our lives that we have control of. But there is no use in trying to change or control other people. The only person each of us has a hope of 'changing' is ourself. We cannot, of course, change who we are, but we can change some important things about ourselves.

Everyone is a complex mixture of different traits and characteristics, and each has its positive and its negative side. For example, being determined is generally a positive good thing, but stubbornness is the negative side of determination.

✓ We can never change what we don't acknowledge. Finding out about AS can help us identity certain traits and aspects within ourselves.

✓ People with AS tend to be individual thinkers. That means they are more likely to work out for themselves what matters and what is important to them.

✓ Anyone – Aspies included – can choose to grow and develop as they go through life.

✓ As we identify specific traits in ourselves, we are in a better position to work out how a particular trait is serving us:

- ○ Does it make life easier or harder (for ourselves and for the people around us)?

- ○ Is it something that needs to be accepted or changed?

✓ As we get to know ourselves better in this way, we can choose to gradually master aspects of ourselves – some traits may need to be managed; others we may want to develop and strengthen.

✓ This may be the start of a task that will last a lifetime, but it is a very worthwhile task. Keep on trying and don't give up!

Meeting challenges makes life interesting. Life would be boring if we didn't have challenges to meet.

COURAGE

When you have AS, you may have more than your fair share of problems to deal with.

✓ Don't run away from problems or ignore them. Do the opposite instead. Face and tackle them – when you really identify and acknowledge a problem, you're about half-way to the solution!

✓ Build and rely on your own individual courage when you are facing problems and challenges.

Facing problems takes courage. By facing problems we discover strength in ourselves that we might not otherwise have known.

ASPERGER SYNDROME – ADVICE FOR LIFE

✓ Whether you are giving or receiving advice – weigh it carefully!

Always be on the lookout for good advice. You never know where you might find it! As the old saying goes, 'You can get a tip from any old duffer!'

SOME GENERAL POSITIVE POINTERS

✓ Be who you are.

✓ Be proud of who you are, including the AS parts.

✓ When you do something you regret, don't wallow in guilt; don't try to blame other people. Take responsibility for your own choices and actions.

✓ Believe in yourself – pursue your passions, but aim to keep balance.

✓ Find your gifts.

✓ Take time to think about other people. Try to appreciate them and find out what matters to them.

✓ Get to know other Aspies.

✓ Try and find out the social rules. Even if you do not see the point in them or agree with them, it can be useful to at least know what they are.

> *Life is a succession of lessons, which must be lived to be understood.*
>
> *Ralph Waldo Emerson*

ATTITUDE

- ✓ Don't expect too much. There will be days when you feel positive and days when you don't.

- ✓ Don't brush problems under the carpet, but don't dwell on them either.

- ✓ See life as a series of choices and learning opportunities. We are choosing all the time, but we need to realise we have choices. We can choose our attitude; and we can choose to learn from our mistakes.

- ✓ Be open and honest – at least with yourself.

- ✓ Focus on finding a way forward or a solution.

> No matter what you meet in life, the one thing you can control is your own attitude.

GREATNESS AND AS

- ✓ Many of the core traits of Asperger Syndrome have been essential in mankind's progress throughout history.

- ✓ Find out about great, famous and gifted people who have made real contributions to the world, and who either had Asperger Syndrome or at least had AS traits. Be inspired by them, but at the same time remember that most people with AS are not so remarkable!

- ✓ Even if it is not obvious, and it takes a long time to find – keep believing in the greatness within yourself.

> *And this above all unto thine own self be true and it shall follow as the day the night – thou can'st not then be false to any man.*
>
> *William Shakespeare*

ASPERGER SYNDROME – 300 POSITIVES (AN A–Z)

ABOUT THE 300 POSITIVES

It is very easy to focus on the downside when you face a difficulty. The idea of the A–Z is that when you come up against a specific issue, you have something to dip into that can offer some alternative, more positive ways of seeing things!

The A–Z sets out in alphabetical order a selection of the challenges, difficulties and issues that are commonly associated with AS. For each topic, only a few sentences are devoted to describing the 'downside' but a number of positive points are listed. The reason for this is that if you have come up against the challenge or difficulty, you already know what the downside is. You could probably write an essay on it yourself, so you don't need to read one!

If you are a person with Asperger Syndrome it should give you some idea of some of the things you might expect, and perhaps you will be able to identify and recognise some things that will apply to yourself. The idea of the A–Z is not only to identify these aspects and traits, but to suggest ways in which these things can be seen positively.

If you don't have AS, but you have someone close to you who does have it, then it will give some clues on what you might expect in a person with AS, and I hope that it will help you understand some of the things that can sometimes seem baffling, and be more positive in how you think about and respond to them.

300 POSITIVES INDEX

ABILITY

The Downside

Compared to other people Aspies find some things extremely easy and some things extremely difficult. In fact the difference is sometimes so extreme that Aspies can be 'gifted' in some areas but have 'special needs' in others. Sometimes people just notice the things Aspies are good at, and expect them to be good at everything. Or the other way round.

Positive Points

✓ Everybody has things that they are good at and things they are not so good at. Don't limit yourself just because you are not naturally good at the same things as everyone else. Find your natural talents and try to develop them. Keep an open mind and be prepared to be surprised.

✓ Sometimes it is obvious where your natural talent lies, because you may have a special interest in some subject, and that can be a good clue. But even if it is not obvious, keep trying to find it out. That can be useful to help you decide how you want to spend your time and even what career you might want to follow.

✓ Some things take more effort than others to learn. But learning is never impossible. When you have Asperger Syndrome you tend to develop at different rates from other people – in some areas more quickly and in some areas more slowly. The good news about that is that over time you may find that you are capable of a lot more than you thought.

✓ Sometimes the things that we find hardest to learn are the ones we get most satisfaction from.

✓ You are not a failure just because you find some things difficult. Effort is what matters.

Everyone has different gifts and abilities. It is what you do with them that matters.

AUTHORITY

The Downside

It is often said that AS children do not seem to have much regard or respect for authority. People in authority in their lives such as teachers and employers tend to see them as defiant and uncooperative.

Positive Points

✓ Aspies do not generally set out to be awkward and defiant. Sometimes the problem is that they have very little grasp of the basic principles of authority or hierarchy.

✓ It can be helpful for both NT's and Aspies to put this into words, for example:

THE BASIC CONCEPT OF AUTHORITY

○ There are all kinds of social systems in the world – families, schools and countries for example; and in order for any of them to run properly there needs to be some person or persons in authority. The people in authority in a social system tend to be the ones who hold positions of both responsibility and power. If things are to run smoothly, it is important that everyone concerned knows and respects authority. That means everybody needs to know who's in charge.

○ In a family, for example, the parents hold responsibility in the sense that they take care of the family and do things like housework, paying the bills and even providing a home. And they hold the power in the sense that they have the right to make certain rules. In a school teachers have responsibility for teaching the class; and they also have the power to make rules within it. The head-teacher has the power to make more rules because he has more responsibility within the school.

✓ It is not always a good idea to just go along with things and do the same thing that other people are doing. Challenging rules is healthy up to a point.

✓ Aspies make us think more about authority than we would otherwise. It can be useful to analyse the reasons for rules.

✓ Aspies can stick to rules very meticulously. This is more likely to happen when:

○ they understand and accept the concept of authority

○ they know very clearly what the rules and consequences are; and

○ that they will be consistently applied.

Anyone who conducts an argument by appealing to authority is not using his intelligence; he is just using his memory.

Leonardo DaVinci

BALANCE

See also the sections on Obsessions and Special interests.

The Downside

Often Aspies find it hard to keep things in balance – their emotions, their interests, their reactions to things. They can get obsessed by things, as in when they have special interests. They are inclined to get things out of proportion, e.g. to get upset about minor things or to find it hard to make decisions, because they see it as much more important than it really is.

Positive Points

✓ There is a fine line between obsession and determination, and determination can be a real positive if channelled into something important.

✓ Sometimes people with AS become obsessive about finding the right answer, or making the right decision. It is worth bearing in mind that there are very often several right answers – there may be more than one way of doing things that will be right.

✓ It is good to be careful about making some decisions even in your own life – i.e. the ones which are life-changing.

✓ It is a good thing to recognise that you have a tendency to be obsessive, because then you can look out for it. When, for example, you see yourself spending a lot of time doing or thinking about one particular thing, you can weigh up whether this is really what you want to be spending your time and energy on.

✓ Be aware of the need for balance in your life.

✓ It is a good idea to assess whether something is really worth getting obsessed about.

✓ Recognise when things are getting out of balance and take practical steps.

> *Personally, I enjoy working about 18 hours a day. Besides the short catnaps I take each day, I average about four to five hours of sleep per night.*
>
> *Thomas Edison*

BRAIN DIFFERENCES

The Downside

People with AS have brains that work differently from typical people. Compared to other people, there are some things they have to work hard to understand and other things they understand more easily.

Positive Points

✓ When you realise, accept and understand that this differ-ence is at the root of Asperger Syndrome, it can give you valuable insights into many of the things about AS that otherwise can seem so mysterious.

✓ Remember – different means just that – different. It does not mean better or worse; and it does not mean stupid.

✓ It is possible to have a more positive and constructive attitude to tackling the difficulties of AS when you identify these differences and understand what effect they have. For example, individuals with AS:

  ○ have brains that naturally need to 'systemise' (that is why they like to put things in order. We see examples of this in train spotters, those who are interested in dinosaurs, or have special interests etc.)

  ○ often need to learn at their own pace (see Learning styles)

- ○ are often visual learners (see Visual thinking).

- ○ can get easily bored by topics that are not of their own choosing (see Motivation)

- ○ tend to be rigid (see Rigidity)

- ○ are often perfectionists, at least in some areas of their lives (see Perfectionism)

- ○ have brains that are more typical of the stereotype of a male than a female; they prefer to sort out problems, even personal ones alone and may withdraw into their 'cave' a lot

- ○ prefer to have information broken down into manageable chunks and written down

- ○ dislike change or the unpredictable (see Rigidity)

- ○ need to 'see the point' for themselves and find it hard to accept anyone else's view of what 'the point' is, so can appear apathetic and unmotivated unless it is on a topic of their own choosing (see Motivation)

- ○ do not appear to have a natural need to comply and fit in (see Conformity).

- ○ may process information at different rates from other people – sometimes more quickly, sometimes more slowly; need time to think (see Learning styles).

- ○ may sometimes find it hard to concentrate (see Concentration).

- ✓ We all process things at different rates.

- ✓ If you process things at different rates it doesn't mean you are stupid.

- ✓ Philosophers are people who take their time thinking. This can make them look and/or feel stupid.

> It is what we use our brains for that matters – what we decide to think about and what we decide not to think about.

CONCENTRATION

The Downside

Sometimes Aspies seem to find it almost impossible to concentrate. Other times, when they are absorbed in something that is of special interest to them, they can concentrate harder and for much longer periods than most people. Problems can arise when they are not concentrating on the things they are supposed to be concentrating on.

Positive Points

✓ When you recognise this trait, you are more likely to find ways that work for you to help you do the things you need to do.

✓ Everyone has their way of thinking, learning and doing things. If you find out what yours is, you will be able to take this into account and do things in a way that suits you (see also Learning styles).

✓ Remember you do have the ability to concentrate well, so even if it is difficult, it is possible to learn to concentrate and apply yourself to things you are not interested in – at least when it is important.

✓ As you get older there are certain advantages in not spending time on things that you don't like. You are less likely to end up in a job you hate for example.

✓ There are certain sensible things that you can do which will give you more control over your concentration levels, such as taking regular exercise and limiting your intake of sugar and caffeine.

✓ If you have problems with concentrating in school, it may be helpful to have an assistant in class to help.

✓ It is really useful to be able to focus hard per se.

✓ When an Aspie finds the right career – one that he likes and is interested in – he can apply himself fully. The route to this may be indicated by his special interest.

> When Isaac Newton was working on a topic that interested him, he would often work right through the night without stopping.

CONFORMITY

The Downside

Most people conform more than Aspies do. That means they follow social rules, both written and unwritten, and they tend to behave in ways that are similar to other people.

Positive Points

✓ If you have AS, you have a unique mindset. That means you are very much your own person.

✓ The world needs both conformists and non-conformists. It is important that people conform or the world would be very chaotic. But sometimes non-conformists are important too.

✓ Non-conformists are often original thinkers, and originality is a good thing (see Original thinking).

✓ Nobody is a complete conformist just as nobody is a complete non-conformist. You can look at different areas of your life and see where you might want to make changes. At the end of the day even though people will try and force you to conform, it is really up to you. (In order to decide, you could take into consideration how important the area is to you and to the people in your life.)

✓ When you are making decisions, it is good to weigh things up and take people's advice, but it is not always a good idea to do things just because other people are doing them.

✓ Many great people come across as eccentric and non-conformists.

✓ Many people who have made significant contributions to the world had views that differed from those of the society in which they lived; for example Winston Churchill, Pablo Picasso, William Shakespeare, Vincent Van Gogh, Mark Twain, H.G. Wells.

✓ Sometimes Aspies can be extreme conformists, by observing carefully what goes on in the social world and having found out what the 'rules' are. (Sometimes extreme conformists are 'hidden Aspies' and may not be diagnosed.)

It takes courage to be different. If everyone was the same it would be a very boring world.

CREATIVITY

The Downside

Sometimes creativity in Aspies can be hidden or unrecognised – perhaps because it is too unusual or too outrageous for other people to be able to appreciate or even relate to, perhaps because someone is hiding or repressing this part of him- or herself.

Positive Points

✓ Creativity is when people express who they are in a free, individual and unique way. It can take many different forms, and it doesn't have to be perfect.

✓ The paintings of Van Gogh and the music of Beethoven may be some of the world's finest examples of creativity – but creativity can come in all sorts of ways.

✓ Creative artists need high levels of energy, determination, focus, all of which are common in people with AS.

✓ Creativity should be fostered and encouraged, but not forced. You may find you are creative in ways you wouldn't expect. Do what you are drawn to do creatively and you will find what is right for you to do.

✓ It is possible to live creatively, for example, when you embark on the path of self-awareness and self-knowledge and you try to improve and change how you behave and relate in the world.

✓ Being creative can encourage and inspire other people to be creative as well.

✓ Creativity is a great way to lift the spirit and relieve depression.

Don't limit what you think of as creativity. Everyone has the potential to be creative.

DEPRESSION

The Downside

It is not unusual for people who have a diagnosis of AS to be prone to depression.

Positive Points

✓ Depression is a normal part of life. Everyone gets depressed at some time of their lives, but it almost always passes.

✓ When you are depressed you may not feel like talking about it, but it can help to talk to someone you trust. Seeking help when you need it is a sign of strength.

✓ There are certain steps you can take to tackle and even overcome depression. See Useful Websites at the back of this book for more information.

✓ It can be helpful to understand the causes of your depression.

✓ Sometimes the reason Aspies get depressed is that they feel they are not doing things right and failing to meet the expectations of other people. The more you understand your Asperger Syndrome the more you realise that this is not true.

✓ Coming through to the other side of depression can make you a better person, and feel better about yourself in some ways, for example:

  ○ You know you can survive tough times.

  ○ You find out that you are stronger, tougher and more resilient than you realise.

  ○ It can give you a new perspective on life.

  ○ It allows you to be more compassionate to other people when they are going through similar difficulties.

- ○ You have more confidence and that allows you to deal better with problems that might come along in the future.

- ✓ There is medication available that can help you through difficult times. Medication can help give you clarity during those times when depression makes things seem hopeless.

- ✓ Depression seems to be part of the price we pay for brilliance and greatness (see below).

> Some of the people who have made great contributions to humanity have suffered from depression, for example Mozart, Michaelangelo and Isaac Newton.

DETERMINATION/STUBBORNNESS

The Downside

People with AS are often very single-minded and to other people this can make them seem awkward and hard to get on with.

Positive Points

- ✓ Aspies themselves tend to see this attribute as a great asset.

- ✓ Determination is a kind of strength.

- ✓ It is needed for success of any kind.

- ✓ Determination will help you achieve your purpose.

- ✓ You need to be determined to achieve anything, especially against the odds.

✓ If people think badly of you, or think you will not be able to achieve much, you can use your determination to prove them wrong.

Many people who have made significant contributions to the world have been people of great determination, for example Winston Churchill, Pablo Picasso, William Shakespeare, Vincent Van Gogh, Mark Twain, H.G. Wells.

DIAGNOSIS

The Downside

Being diagnosed with AS can cause various types of difficulty. Some people who have AS never get diagnosed at all; some get diagnosed late in life, and some people do not like the idea of having AS.

Positive Points

✓ Finding out that you have AS can make you feel better about yourself and can help you understand more about:

   ○ who you really are

   ○ why you behave in certain ways and

   ○ some of the difficulties you have had.

✓ When you find out you have AS it can help you stop feeling bad about some of the 'mistakes' you feel you have made.

✓ It is easier for you to be true to yourself.

✓ You realise there are plenty of other people in the world who have AS, which can make you feel less alone and different.

✓ You can begin to realise that any feelings you might have had that you are stupid or a failure were wrong.

✓ When other people become aware of your diagnosis, it can help them to understand you better and they may make some changes in how they deal with you that might make things run more smoothly.

✓ Once you know you have AS, you can start to find out more about it.

✓ AS tends to run in families, so when one person in the family gets a diagnosis, it is not uncommon for someone else to get a diagnosis as well, perhaps at a later stage. That way hidden Aspies come to light as well.

✓ When you find out more about AS, it can be interesting and fun to speculate about other people who may be 'hidden Aspies' – either people you know or famous people.

✓ It can also be fun to look for AS traits in your family.

One Aspie who did not receive a diagnosis until he was an adult told me 'I feel so much better about myself since I got my diagnosis. It was a relief to understand the reason for so many decisions I made in my life that seemed stupid at the time. The main advantage of the diagnosis for me is that I don't feel stupid and guilty any more.'

DISABILITY

The Downside

Some people call AS a disability, but some people do not agree that it is right to call it a disability.

Positive Points

✓ If AS is a disability, it is mostly a social disability, because it affects the way Aspies relate to other people. You can apply yourself to learning social skills, and if you are determined, you will improve over time, so that things can improve for you as you get older.

✓ The social disability can be a problem when you are at school age, because you have to spend a lot of time with people you have little in common with. The good news is that school does not last forever; and as you get older you become freer to choose who you want to spend your time with. You are also more likely to meet people with whom you have more in common.

✓ Being disabled means that there are some things you cannot do, or that you only do with great difficulty. On the other hand when you have AS there are often other things that you are able to do much better than the average person.

✓ Having AS does not mean that you are stupid or mentally retarded. It just means that your brain works differently to most people's so that certain things are easier for you and other things are harder for you than they are for most people.

✓ Certain things will be difficult for you if you have AS, but even though these things may never come easily to you, there is a lot that you can do to help yourself if you are determined.

✓ The fact that AS is considered to be a disability may mean that you will be in a better position to get help and benefits that may make life easier for you.

✓ Calling AS a disability may encourage people to take it more seriously.

✓ Even if it is a disability, there are much worse disabilities about; and you are in a good position to appreciate and empathise with people who have a more severe disability.

> *You can overcome the things about AS that make life difficult if you are determined enough. You just need to keep trying and never give up.*
>
> *Kenneth Hall*

EMPLOYMENT

The Downside

Many people with AS end up unemployed or else in jobs for which they are overqualified (in terms of ability).

Aspies may find a lot of things about working in a conventional job very difficult – working 9–5, being part of a team, following instructions that they do not see the point of, as well as the social aspect of the job.

Positive Points

✓ These days things are improving so that there is more chance of Aspies finding a job that suits them – particularly because computers have become more popular and Aspies are often very good with computers.

✓ The key is often finding out what you like doing and finding out how to make a career out of that somehow. If you have a special interest, that may provide a clue.

✓ Many jobs involving computers do not involve the things that Aspies find difficult, for example there is less need for face-to-face meetings with people when you are dealing with them on-line.

✓ When Aspies find a job that suits them, they tend to have certain qualities that are very useful – honesty, loyalty, diligence, determination and attention to detail.

✓ The attention to detail that is typical of AS can be very useful in some jobs.

✓ The fact that Aspies are unlikely to be very interested in the social aspect of the job means that they are more likely to focus their time and energy on the job itself.

✓ These days there is more scope for flexibility within work – for example part-time working – and this can suit Aspies better.

✓ It is always possible for Aspies to create their own job – especially via the internet.

✓ Remember it is not only Aspies who have problems with their job. A lot of people do not enjoy their careers, but a good income is useful to enable a good standard of living.

✓ If you can be realistic about what type of job you would like, you are more likely to be successful.

One Aspie used a special interest in diamonds to pursue a qualification in gemmology, which is a useful route into a career as a diamond grader! So sometimes special interests that seem obscure and unlikely can turn out to be a path to a career opportunity.

FEELING DIFFERENT

The Downside

No two people are the same, and in reality we are all different from each other to some extent. When you are aware of this difference, it can make you feel like an outsider and as if you don't belong. People with AS experience this feeling to an intense degree.

Positive Points

✓ If you are an Aspie, the truth is that you are different from most other people – but that's OK.

✓ The feeling of being different or as if you are 'on the wrong planet' is something that all Aspies experience from time to time, so you are not alone in this. In fact everyone feels a bit like this at least occasionally.

✓ It is good to be your own person. Some people would secretly like to feel free enough to be different like an Aspie.

✓ Everyone wants to 'belong' sometimes, and when you are different it is harder for you to belong. When an Aspie is true to himself, it may make him stand out. It takes courage to be different.

✓ Being different can be a blessing.

✓ The world needs a diversity of people who are set apart from the norm. Many great and remarkable people have gone through life feeling different.

✓ It would be a very boring world if we were all alike!

✓ The feeling of being different can be a catalyst to compassion and creativity.

As a child Hans Christian Anderson felt different from everyone around him and suffered a lot of ridicule and bullying. Many of the characters in his stories, such as The Ugly Duckling and Pinocchio, are portrayed as having feelings of being different and alienated.

FRIENDSHIP

The Downside

Often people with Asperger Syndrome have difficulties with making and keeping friends.

Positive Points

- ✓ School can be stressful for children with AS. The good news about this is that things can improve over time as they:

    - ○ learn more about themselves and become more confident and happy about who they are

    - ○ learn how the social world works and develop their social skills

    - ○ develop their own interests and find people who share those interests.

- ✓ These days a lot of people – whether they have AS or not – have on-line friends and spend long periods of time 'talking' to them, using programmes such as instant messengers. The on-line community can work well for people with Asperger Syndrome.

- ✓ If you are lucky enough to become the friend of an Aspie, you will probably find him to be an interesting person, loyal, straight and on the level.

- ✓ Organisations such as NAS run Befriending Schemes and Social Groups which can be helpful for Aspies.

✓ Sometimes Aspies make friends with other Aspies. This can work very well because they can understand each other.

Books, like friends, should be few and well chosen.
Samuel Paterson

GETTING IT WRONG

The Downside

Aspies tend to be perfectionists, and hate to feel they are getting things wrong. They are very vulnerable to this feeling, particularly because of their difficulties with social skills.

Positive Points

✓ If you think you get it wrong all the time, take it from me – you don't! It is just that as an Aspie you give yourself a very hard time any time you do get it wrong and sometimes you forget to pay attention to all the things you get right.

✓ When you get something wrong, let it go and try not to do the same thing again.

✓ Break it down and see where you went wrong.

✓ If you find it hard to get something right, don't be afraid to ask for help.

✓ Accept that it can take you longer than others to get some things right.

✓ Let yourself off. Realise that when you get certain things wrong it may be a symptom of AS; and when you feel extremely bad about it, that may be a symptom of AS as well.

✓ When you get things out of proportion, try not to take it too seriously. Have a laugh instead!

> Everyone makes mistakes – that's why they put rubbers on pencils!

GIFTS

Positive Points

✓ Sometimes people with AS can have unusual and special gifts and talents.

✓ Even though it is not easy to figure out exactly what the relationship is, there does seem to be some sort of association between AS and giftedness.

✓ Even if they do not have AS, or they have never been diagnosed with it, it is very common for people who are highly gifted to show symptoms of AS. For example they often seem intense, can come across as eccentric and tend to have social difficulties.

✓ It is hard to say how many people with AS are gifted because sometimes their gifts may go unrecognised. For example, they may be 'hidden Aspies' and sometimes people who hide their AS also hide their gifts.

✓ Some Aspies can be gifted in areas which need a very logical brain – for example computer programming and maths.

✓ Some Aspies can be creatively gifted and be great artists, for example. Many world-famous creatively gifted people show traits of AS.

✓ There are many types of gifts. Aspies may have obscure interests, and these may indicate where their area of giftedness lies.

✓ Some gifts are late to develop and late to show themselves. Do not assume that you are not gifted because you have not yet found out where your gifts and passion lie.

✓ People have interesting views about AS. Some people say that AS is a form of giftedness, even though it brings its own difficulties. Some say that Asperger Syndrome is part of the price that is paid for greatness.

Everyone has some sort of gift. Keep trying till you find what you are good at.

GUILT AND SHAME

The Downside

Many Aspies, especially those who do not receive diagnosis until late in life, go through life carrying a heavy burden of guilt and shame about decisions they have made, things they have done or not done, and an embarrassment about who they really are.

Positive Points

✓ Shame and guilt are like extreme forms of responsibility, in the sense that you feel overly responsible for things in your life. Responsibility is a good thing, because it means you are aware of how your behaviour is affecting other people and you are trying to make good choices.

✓ Try to be someone who takes responsibility for the things you do, but try to keep your sense of responsibility in balance, and don't overdo it by going to the other extreme!

✓ If you know you have done something you shouldn't have, the first thing to do is admit it, at least to yourself. You might then decide to apologise and make amends, but don't be ashamed of who you are.

✓ Remember – mistakes are learning opportunities. When you make a mistake, see it as an opportunity to do things differently the next time. Or at least to try.

✓ There may be things you want to change about how you behave. Changing your behaviour may not be easy, but the fact that you are prepared to try is very admirable.

✓ Never let anyone make you feel you need to change who you are. Be proud of who you are and do your best.

> The diaries of some great writers who also displayed other AS traits, for example WB Yeats, were full of self-criticism. Lewis Carroll's diaries reveal that much of the time he thought of himself as worthless.

HELP FOR PARENTS AND CARERS

The Downside

When there is someone in the family with AS, it can put a lot of pressure on the whole family. This section is mainly for people who are thinking of helping out – perhaps friends or people in the extended family network.

Positive Points

TO HELPERS

- ✓ Helpers may be in a position to make things better by taking some of the pressure off the family.

- ✓ Parents and carers will probably be very glad of any help they can get. Often what they need most is a break.

- ✓ It may take trial and error to find out just how much help and support is needed.

- ✓ Try to provide support without judgement.

- ✓ The best type of help is practical help, but the more you understand AS the better.

- ✓ Remember your role is to help and not to fix.

- ✓ Often the best help of all is the gift of your time.

TO PARENTS AND CARERS

- ✓ You do not have to cope with everything on your own. Aim to create a helpful and flexible team (ideally formed of family, friends and professionals) around you. See Useful Websites at the back of this book for further information.

- ✓ Talk to professionals and experts and don't be afraid to speak up when you are struggling and need help.

- ✓ Although you need to be selective about what help you accept, think twice before turning help away.

> *People seldom refuse help, if one offers it in the right way.*
>
> A.C. Benson

HELP FOR PEOPLE WITH AS

The Downside

Giving a person with AS too much help can hold him back from helping himself, and it can come across as patronising. Giving a person with AS too little help can leave him floundering.

Positive Points

✓ There is a lot more recognition and awareness about AS these days than there ever was, and this is improving all the time. That is a good thing because it means there is more help available than there used to be.

✓ Try to distinguish what is helpful from what is unhelpful, and keep an open mind.

✓ You may need less help as time goes by, or you may need different types of help, and it is important that you communicate this with the people who are helping you.

✓ Asking for help when you need it is a mature and sensible thing to do.

✓ When you accept help, you can learn new things and gradually learn to manage with less help.

✓ Try to get a balance between too much and too little help and communicate with people clearly about how much help you think you need.

✓ You may be in a position to help other people with similar difficulties as yours at some later date.

HEROISM AND AS

The Downside

Aspies can find it hard to relate to other people and often come across to outsiders as 'rude, gauche and arrogant', and they tend to think of themselves in a negative way as well. So it is hard for them to think of themselves as any kind of 'heroes'.

Positive Points

✓ A hero is somebody who

  ○ is admired for outstanding qualities or achievements or

  ○ has shown an admirable quality such as great courage or strength of character.

By this definition Aspies certainly are some of life's real heroes.

(In fact if you think about it, there are often heroic qualities in the people who take care of them, especially AS parents, as well!)

✓ Usually Aspies want very much to 'get it right' and to do the right thing in life.

✓ There is a lot to be admired about the traits that are at the very core of AS – Aspies are usually interesting, honest, original and individual.

✓ People who get to know individual Aspies and to understand more about AS, often end up admiring them and seeing them as some of the genuine 'heroes' of life.

✓ Aspies have a lot to cope with in a world that seems alien to them in many ways. It takes a lot of courage and determination to:

  ○ learn things you find hard to learn or don't see the point of, but which other people think are easy and obvious

  ○ rise above it whenever you are misjudged. (People are sometimes intolerant because they don't understand how an intelligent person finds it hard to learn social 'rules' that seem easy and obvious to them.)

✓ Many aspects of the social system and in particular the education system do not suit them – they tend to bring out the worst in the individual with Asperger Syndrome. The ability to cope, adapt and rise above this could well be described as everyday heroism.

> *Our greatest glory consists not in never falling, but in rising every time we fall.*
>
> **Confucius**

HONESTY

The Downside

When Aspies get on the wrong side of people, strangely enough the reason is often that they have been 'too honest'.

Positive Points

✓ Most Aspies seem to be more honest than typical people. Even though this can make them seem tactless, rude or blunt sometimes, overall honesty is a good thing.

✓ Most people tell lies because they want to fit in and conform, but it usually does not occur to an Aspie to tell a lie.

✓ When Aspies come across as tactless, rude or blunt, they usually do not mean to cause any offence.

✓ Most people do not realise how many little lies and white lies they tell until they stop and analyse it. (For example they might tell a lie to please someone by saying they like a present they have just received.) The honesty of an Aspie can be a challenge to society.

✓ The honesty of an Aspie can be inspiring for other people.

✓ When people are honest and direct at least you know where you stand and there is less room for miscommunication.

✓ Even when Aspies tell lies, they are usually not very clever or skilful at it – and overall it is a good thing not to be good at lying.

✓ Some people secretly wish they could be as honest as an Aspie.

✓ It takes courage to be honest.

✓ If everyone was honest, it would surely be a much better world!

Honesty is the first chapter in the book of wisdom.
Thomas Jefferson

INADEQUACY

The Downside

The world seems often to be asking Aspies to do things that they do not find easy – especially things that require social skills. This is one of the things that can cause feelings of inadequacy.

Positive Points

✓ The feeling of inadequacy usually comes about just because you don't do well at the things that other people value. But not everything that the mainstream values is really that valuable.

✓ Being an Aspie means you will be good at some things and bad at others, but the world is built on diversity.

✓ Try and focus on the things you are good at, and accept yourself for who you are.

✓ Sometimes it can be helpful to put yourself in situations that challenge you and take you out of your comfort zone. This can help build up your confidence.

> *Whatever you are from nature, keep to it; never desert your own line of talent... Be what Nature intended you for, and you will succeed; be anything else, and you will be ten thousand times worse than nothing.*
>
> *Sydney Smith*

INDIVIDUALITY

The Downside

Aspies tend to be different, individual and original – and this in itself can make life difficult!

Positive Points

✓ It is a wonderful thing to be 'an individual' because it means you have the courage to be yourself.

✓ Some Aspies see this as one of the most positive aspects of being an Aspie.

✓ Everyone is an individual in a way, but most people have a need to fit in and be like the people around them. Aspies do not need this so much and that allows them to be individuals in a truer sense.

✓ The need to fit in is one of the reasons that society ends up with conventions and traditions and these are good at binding people into groups. But it is a good thing for conventions and traditions to be challenged sometimes too, because binding people into groups can separate them from other groups at the same time – which is one of the causes of conflict in the world.

✓ It is good to stand out from the crowd sometimes.

✓ Being an individual makes you an interesting person.

✓ Being an individual means you are more likely to make decisions because they are right for you rather than because you want to do the same as other people.

✓ Great artists, writers, poets and innovators who produce interesting work are always individuals.

✓ The individuals in society often become trend setters and taste makers.

If you want to be original, just be yourself! No two people are exactly alike.

LEARNING STYLES

The Downside

Everybody has a slightly different way of learning. When you have Asperger Syndrome, the way in which you learn things can be quite different from the way in which most other people learn them.

Positive Points

✓ Although Aspies are good learners, they often have untypical ways of learning. Aspies may, for example:

   ○ learn some things unusually quickly and some unusually slowly

   ○ learn things better by seeing them than by hearing them

- ○ understand things better when they figure them out for themselves rather than have someone tell them

- ○ find it very hard to learn things that are of no interest to them

- ○ have an unusual concentration span (see Concentration).

✓ It is good to find out your own learning style, because learning is important – it not just something that happens at school; it is something we do all our lives.

✓ When you find something hard to learn, don't give up.

✓ As you get older, there is more scope for the kind of learning that is better suited to an Aspie. For example:

- ○ There is more scope for specialised learning, so you have more chance of focusing on the subjects that interest you and dropping the ones that don't.

- ○ It becomes easier to follow your own agenda about the subjects you are really interested in learning, and there is plenty of choice in adult education.

✓ You are not stupid because you have a different way of learning things.

✓ These days there is great scope for learning all sorts of interesting things via the internet.

✓ There is a lot more recognition about AS and about different learning styles than there used to be.

The way I learn best is to figure things out for myself. I don't like to learn things by being told them.
                                                        Kenneth Hall

LONELINESS

The Downside

Sometimes Aspies enjoy their own company, but sometimes they feel an acute sense of loneliness and isolation.

Positive Points

✓   It is good to have times of solitude as well as time to be with people. The ideal balance would allow room for both.

✓   Most people do not have enough space and solitude in their lives.

✓   Solitude allows you to retreat from the world of noise and confusion.

✓   Being a loner has its advantages. For example you are more likely to be creative when you have time and space to be alone. Poets and musicians need solitude, for example.

✓   Being a bit of a loner can help you appreciate the nicer people in life!

✓   In order to discover the nature of yourself and the world you live in, you need to embark on an inner journey. You need solitude for this.

> *The individual has always had to struggle to keep from being overwhelmed by the tribe. If you try it, you will be lonely often, and sometimes frightened. But no price is too high to pay for the privilege of owning yourself.*
>
> *Friedrich Nietzsche*

MARRIAGE/PRIMARY RELATIONSHIPS

The Downside

People with AS find relationships difficult and they also find it hard to live according to 'normal' expectations – both these things can cause problems when it comes to partnerships such as marriage.

Positive Points

✓ Aspies do generally try hard to do the right thing and meet the expectations of a partner.

✓ They are often very loyal partners.

✓ Marriage and marriage-type partnerships sometimes work very well if either:

    ◦ you meet a partner who is very tolerant and understands AS and how it affects you, or

    ◦ you meet another Aspie who is very similar to you and the two of you have a lot in common.

> *There is nothing nobler or more admirable than when two people who see eye to eye keep house as man and wife, confounding their enemies and delighting their friends.*
>
> *Homer*

MENTAL HEALTH

The Downside

Although the nature of the connection is not clear, there appears to be a link of some sort between AS and mental health problems.

Positive Points

- ✓ There are certain steps you can take to foster good mental health. See Useful Websites at the back of this book for more information.

- ✓ AS is not in itself a mental illness.

- ✓ Mental illness in not inevitable just because you have AS.

- ✓ The link between AS and mental illness is at least partly due to the fact that the world finds it very hard to adjust to Aspies. It is possible to improve this by raising awareness about AS in society generally.

- ✓ The link is also at least partly due to the fact that Aspies finds it very hard to adjust to the world. It is possible to improve this too.

- ✓ You can take a certain amount of responsibility for your own mental health just as you can take a certain amount of responsibility for your physical health.

- ✓ If you can find a living environment that is right for you that can prove very helpful.

- ✓ Self-awareness and knowledge of AS can be very helpful in this.

- ✓ The fact that you have particular difficulties does not make you mentally ill.

- ✓ If a doctor does diagnose you as having a mental illness, there is no shame in that. The diagnosis can be the first step towards getting you the help that you need.

- ✓ Mental illness can be overcome, and coming through mental illness can make you a better person. You may become:

  - ○ stronger

  - ○ more compassionate

- ○ more tolerant
- ○ less judgemental
- ○ in a better position to understand and help others.

MOTIVATION

The Downside

Aspies are often said to be 'hard to motivate'. This can make life difficult for the people around them, especially parents and teachers.

Positive Points

- ✓ It is not true to say that Aspies have poor motivation. They can have very strong motivation when it concerns either:
  - ○ something that they want or that is of special interest to them, or
  - ○ something they see the point of.
- ✓ When Aspies are genuinely motivated about something, they can put enormous focus and energy into it. When it comes to the subject area that specially interests them, their application can be amazing.
- ✓ If you can find a way to make a career out of something you are really interested in, this can be the key to happiness and success.
- ✓ When you find what you really want to do with your life, you will be able to put a lot of time and energy into it. If you are not sure what that is, keep persevering. You will find it eventually.
- ✓ Sometimes children with AS find it hard to see the point in what they are expected to do. But there is usually a reason for the things that people in authority ask you to do –

they are generally not setting out to make life difficult for you personally.

✓ The more you understand and accept the basic principles of authority the less difficult you will find it to do things that seem pointless to you (see the section on Authority).

✓ Even though it is not always appropriate, it can sometimes be a good idea to ask the reason why you are being asked to do something, as long as you are polite about it.

✓ Even if you do not know the reason, or you think the reason is not a good one, it is good to admit that you might be wrong about it.

> Motivation is often more important than talent. When a person has a little bit of talent plus a lot of motivation, he can sometimes accomplish more than if had a lot of talent but very little motivation.

OBSESSIONS

See also Special interests and Rigidity.

The Downside

The Asperger brain is very prone to be obsessive, for example when a special interest in something is developed. Having an obsessive mind can be difficult, because you can get fixed on one thing, making it hard for you to move on to thinking about something else that might be important.

Positive Points

✓ Special interests can be a lot of fun.

✓ Obsessions and special interests can lead to a satisfying career.

✓ When you are obsessed about something that is socially acceptable or that other people find interesting, obsessions can help you to be very successful in life.

✓ Obsessive tendencies are often associated with great achievement.

Lewis Carroll was obsessive about keeping lists and writing letters. He sent and received a total of 98,721 letters in his last 35 years.

ORGANISATION/EXECUTIVE FUNCTION

The Downside

Aspies need order in their lives, but it can be very hard for them to create it, and so they can come across as very chaotic and disorganised. They find it very hard to 'get things done' and complete plans and projects (what is known as 'executive function'). At the opposite extreme, sometimes Aspies can be extremely organised, or even controlling, at least in some areas.

Positive Points

✓ A lot of people find it hard to organise themselves at times.

✓ There are all sorts of things you can do to help make your life more organised. Find out which ones work for you.

✓ Everyone has to find methods to help organise their lives. That is why people use diaries and lists, for example.

✓ If you find something very hard to organise, keep trying. You will get there in the end.

✓ Over time you can develop structures and routines that work for you and make it easier for you to manage things in your life.

✓ If you find it hard to manage very important things in your life, you may be able to get help with them.

✓ Try your best to be organised, but try not to get too hung up on it. Being a bit messy may just be part of who you are.

Some very remarkable people were 'Asperger-ish' in this. At one extreme, for example, Einstein was considered to be very messy, whereas Jonathan Swift was extreme in his orderliness and was very fond of making lists to help him organise his life.

ORIGINAL THINKING

See also Individuality and Feeling different.

The Downside

Aspies tend to be different in the way that they think about things. Other people can find that difficult and challenging at times.

Positive Points

✓ Many people with AS see this as one of the most valuable things about Asperger Syndrome and the one that they would least like to change about themselves.

✓ Original thinking allows you to come up with new ways of looking at things – and that can be interesting and refreshing.

✓   The world needs original thinkers – for example inventors and philosophers need to be original thinkers.

✓   Many great and respected people today and throughout history have been original thinkers.

Isaac Newton is a good example of an original thinker. He became interested in gravity by looking at a commonplace phenomenon, namely an apple falling from a tree, and thinking of it in an original way.

PAINFUL FEELINGS

The Downside

Aspies can struggle with some painful feelings as they go through life. Some Aspies do not say much about how they feel, either because they find it hard to know themselves, or because they just don't think of telling anyone. Others can be over the top in telling anyone who will listen in an exaggerated and dramatic way!

Positive Points

✓   Understand that as an Aspie your feelings may be intense; don't let them dominate your life or disable you from moving forward.

✓   Have a look at the individual section below that deal with the following painful feelings:

    o   different (see Feeling Different; Individuality, Conformity; Diagnosis)

    o   embarrassed or ashamed (see Getting it wrong; Guilt)

    o   guilty (see Guilt and Shame)

- ○ inadequate (see Inadequacy)
- ○ lonely (see Loneliness; Depression; Space and Solitude)
- ○ rejection (see Rejection; Loneliness; Depression)
- ○ stupid (see Stupidity, feelings of).

Painful feelings always pass, and there is often a lot to learn from experiencing them. And remember – they are rarely as bad as they seem. It only takes one cloud to block out the sun!

PERFECTIONISM

The Downside

People with Asperger Syndrome can get upset if things are not 'perfect' – or what they see to be perfect.

Positive Points

- ✓ If you are perfectionist about something at least it shows that that thing means a lot to you.
- ✓ Being a perfectionist can give you very high standards about things.
- ✓ As long as it does not get out of balance, it can be a big plus to have high standards.
- ✓ It can be a real asset in many careers.
- ✓ Many artists and craftsmen are perfectionists.
- ✓ Great attention to details can produce some outstanding work.

The paintings of Michaelangelo are a great example of attention to detail and perfectionism. There is an interesting anecdote about him in relation to this, which says that he once visited a shoemaker friend to ask him how many eyelets (lace holes) were in a particular type of shoe, for a painting that he was working on at the time. The shoemaker was surprised at his concern over something so trivial, and referred to the matter as just a 'trifle'.

The artist's answer was as follows: 'Trifles make perfection – and perfection is no trifle.'

REJECTION

The Downside

Because people with AS are often excluded, and because there is often so much of a focus on trying to change and improve aspects of their behaviour (which they sometimes see as part of their identity) they are vulnerable to feelings of rejection.

Positive Points

✓ The feeling of rejection is one that everybody in the world feels from time to time, so you are not alone.

✓ People may not include you because you don't join in or communicate much. It may not be that they are setting out to reject you.

✓ When people want you to change your behaviour, that does not necessarily mean they are trying to change or reject who you are.

✓ Understand that if people do reject you, the reason may not be personal. There is a strong desire in humans to be part of a group and feel they belong and that is why they sometimes do not like associating with people who are different and who do not seem to be part of their group.

✓ Even if other people reject you, do not reject yourself.

✓ When you know what the feeling of rejection feels like, you can try to make sure you never do anything to make anyone else feel rejected.

✓ If you are rejected by some people, it can help you really appreciate people who accept you and are warm and loving towards you.

✓ Finding your own place in the world takes perseverance and courage. When you do this you will find you draw upon strengths you didn't even know you had.

The paintings of Vincent Van Gogh were rejected during his lifetime and only began to receive recognition as great works of art many years later.

RIGIDITY

The Downside

People who have AS generally find it hard to be flexible. They need the world to be predictable and get anxious and upset when things change.

Positive Points

✓ There is generally a link between anxiety and rigidity – the more anxious you are the more rigid you tend to be. If you can keep your anxiety levels from getting too high, you will find it easier to cope when unpredictable things happen.

✓ Everyone finds change difficult.

✓ It is possible to train yourself to become less rigid over time.

✓ People who are rigid tend also to be determined, loyal and not easily led by others.

✓ Aspies often have very set and definite views, which can make them people of high principle and morality.

✓ There are some things that it is important to be rigid about.

✓ When Aspies seem to be rigid in an argument, it may be because their mind works in a rigid way. It is probably not because they are setting out to be annoying.

Philip of Spain (1527–1598), a remarkable king who displayed many symptoms of Asperger Syndrome, had a diet so rigid that he got a dispensation from the Pope saying he didn't have to fast on the ground that a change to his routine might damage his health!

SCHOOL

The Downside
School can be very stressful for children with AS and their parents.

Positive Points

✓ These days there is a lot more understanding about AS in schools; and it is growing all the time.

✓ Although some AS children can be challenging for teachers to deal with, they may also be seen as colourful, interesting characters – by their classmates anyway!

✓ The individuality of some AS children means they may be less easily led than typical children.

✓ If you do not do well at school, there are other routes to a good, satisfying career and business success.

✓ Many people who found school very difficult went on to become successful and world famous in many fields.

✓ The rebellious streak that is often in AS children is necessary for reform and social change.

✓ Even if you absolutely hate school, it is possible to use the AS determination to get through and do as well as you can.

✓ There are schools these days which are better suited to pupils with AS, so there is more possibility of finding a school that suits you.

✓ Try not to let it get to you. School days do not last forever, don't forget!

Mozart, Beethoven, Lewis Carroll and Einstein are just a few examples of people who found their school days very difficult.

SENSORY ISSUES

The Downside

Aspies tend to feel certain things either more or less keenly than other people, or they may feel them differently. They can also become upset by certain sensations that would not bother other people, for example they may be sensitive to certain smells, sounds and lights.

Positive Points

✓ It can be interesting to feel the world in a different way to other people. For example some musicians hear and 'feel' music to an intense degree, and this deep appreciation can apply to other art forms as well.

✓ When you get to know what sensations might be upsetting you, you can learn to avoid those things as much as possible.

✓ If you tell people what is upsetting you, they also can take steps to help you avoid those things.

Donna Williams is an author who has written extensively about her life as an individual with Asperger Syndrome. She has extremely unusual sensory experiences, sometimes being able to 'see' sound for example.

SOCIAL SKILLS

The Downside

Aspies tend to have poor social skills. Sometimes they can come across as 'rude, gauche and arrogant' although it is also possible for them to mask their difficulties by using various strategies.

Positive Points

✓ Although other people can find it hard to understand this difficulty, awareness is growing all the time.

✓ When Aspies break 'social rules' they usually do not mean to. They do not generally set out to cause offence.

✓ Sometimes an Aspie causes offence by breaking a 'hidden' social rule – i.e. one that people follow without realising they are doing it. This creates an opportunity for them to bring the rule to light and think about how important the rule really is, and why.

✓ Sometimes when an Aspie breaks the social rules it means that he has been honest in a situation where most people would have either said nothing or told a white lie. Even though this can cause trouble, honesty is in itself a good and refreshing thing.

✓ When Aspies break the social rules they can come across as tactless – but even if tactlessness is uncomfortable for other people, it can be good for people to know where they stand.

✓ When a person who is unskilful socially does develop friendships, those friendships can be very real and important.

✓ If more people were like Aspies, there would be scope for more honest communication.

✓ We can learn a lot from being direct and honest.

✓ It may not be easy for Aspies to learn social skills, but it is possible if they are open to learning, get help and are determined enough.

Isaac Newton had poor social skills. He seldom left his room and when he was with other people he usually didn't contribute much to the conversation.

SPACE AND SOLITUDE

See also the section on Loneliness.

The Downside

Aspies often need a lot of space and solitude, so they tend to spend a lot of time alone. Whenever they do, it can sometimes be hard for other people to know whether they are lonely or whether they are choosing to be alone because they need space.

Positive Points

✓ Times of solitude can be good for you, and they can help to relieve stress.

✓ Everyone needs times of space and solitude, whether they have Asperger Syndrome or not, although the amount they need will vary from person to person. As you get to know the right amount for you personally, you can then weave this into the fabric of your life.

✓ Let other people know when you think you need space, but try to agree in advance how much time alone you might need.

✓ Having the right amount of space and solitude will not mean hiding from the world – it will allow you to wind down and feel calm and relaxed.

✓ Times of solitude are necessary for deep thinking and self-discovery.

Mozart and Lewis Carroll are both examples of people who needed a lot of space and solitude. Lewis Carroll's life was lonely and isolated and he had no interest in small talk of any kind. Mozart was a withdrawn child who did not play games with other children.

SPECIAL INTERESTS

See also the section on Obsessions.

The Downside

Aspies very often develop special interests. Sometimes these can be on narrow and obscure areas, and they can become all-absorbing.

Positive Points

✓ Aspies can develop very deep and detailed knowledge on areas which are of special interest to them. This can be fascinating and very useful for other people.

✓ Special interests can lead to new discoveries and realisations.

✓ Aspies usually find their special interests satisfying and fun.

✓ Spending time on your special interests can help you feel better, and they can help to relieve anxiety and stress.

✓ Special interests can lead to a rewarding and enjoyable career.

✓ If you can find other people who share your special interest, that can be a route to social success.

✓ Many people with special interests have gone on to achieve great progress.

Many of Newton's achievements would not have been possible without his special interest in physics and optical research. He did have other special interests as well however – for example biblical chronology and numerology.

STUPIDITY (FEELINGS OF)

The Downside

People with AS hate to feel they are 'stupid' but as a result of the difficulties that are associated with AS, they often feel this way.

Positive Points

- ✓ Everyone feels stupid sometimes. Aspies are not alone in this.

- ✓ Part of the diagnostic criteria for AS is that the person should be of at least normal intelligence. Logically speaking therefore, no Aspie can be stupid.

- ✓ There are many different types of intelligence, and everyone is more intelligent about some things than others.

- ✓ Feeling a bit stupid at times can be better than being arrogant and superior.

- ✓ It is good to recognise you are prone to feeling stupid, because then you can challenge the feeling by telling yourself it is not true.

- ✓ It can be helpful to identify and make a list of the things you are good at and the things you have achieved, that show your intelligence.

- ✓ Many of the world's great thinkers such as Einstein and Newton were originally thought of as stupid or mediocre.

- ✓ Stupidity is like madness – in this way at least: they say that if you were really mad, you would never believe you were mad. In the same way, if you were really stupid, you would never believe you were stupid – so the very fact that you feel stupid sometimes proves that you are not!

Hans Christian Anderson's headmaster told him he was a stupid boy and that no one would ever want to read his writing.

TACT

The Downside

Aspies are often perceived as blunt and tactless, for example by saying things which make other people feel uncomfortable. This can cause embarrassment, isolation and judgement.

Positive Points

✓ Usually when Aspies say something tactless it is done unintentionally. They have just broken one of the unwritten rules about what is appropriate to say.

✓ Tact and diplomacy are useful because they help things run more smoothly between people. Part of how this works is that people tell what are known as 'white lies' which are statements that are untrue but are about things which are unimportant. White lies are often told in order to stop someone getting hurt or upset by the truth. The advantage when someone is tactless is that there are no lies and everyone knows exactly where they stand.

✓ Nobody is completely tactful. Everyone says things that they realise later they shouldn't have, from time to time.

✓ When Aspies are straight and direct it can be very refreshing. It is especially refreshing when an Aspie meets another Aspie and they are straight and direct with each other. Neither of them is having to guess what the other really means and each of them can depend on what the other says to be reliable and true.

✓ Some people secretly wish they could be as honest and direct as an Aspie.

✓ Sometimes Aspies put into words what other people are thinking but do not want to say.

✓ Aspies can challenge all of us to be more honest and direct.

✓ When social rules are explained to Aspies very clearly, they can learn to be tactful and diplomatic.

✓ Sometimes when Aspies are tactless it can be very funny.

> *Tact is the art of making a point without making an enemy.*
>
> *Isaac Newton*

VISUAL THINKING

The Downside

Aspies generally are visual thinkers. That means it can be hard for them to understand, process and remember things which are not, for example, written down.

Positive Points

✓ Everybody's brain processes things differently. There is no right or wrong in this. The important thing is to be aware of it.

✓ When you talk to someone with AS and he seems to not listen, not understand or forget things, this does not mean that he is stupid or unreliable. It may simply mean that he needs to be able to see it rather than hear it.

✓ Temple Grandin wrote a book called *Thinking in Pictures* in which she explained how her mind worked. The fact that she was a visual thinker helped her as a designer, because she was able to visualise what she was designing so fully.

✓ Everybody thinks visually to some extent, so it is easy to understand the concept. For example, people use diaries and calendars which let them see time passing, and they write things like to-do lists because it is helpful to be able to see what they have to do.

✓ When you recognise how the AS brain works, you can take this into account to help you understand, learn and remember things (e.g. you can use visual aids such as lists and diagrams).

Temple Grandin, a world-renowned professor and expert in animal science, wrote a book entitled *Thinking in Pictures* in which she explains how she sees the world. She used her ability to 'think in pictures' to help her design humane animal handling equipment.

ASPIE QUOTATIONS

While I was doing research for this book, I interviewed many people who are involved in the world of Asperger Syndrome – Aspies, parents, teachers and so on. This section contains a sample of quotations taken from these interviews.

QUOTATIONS FROM PARENTS, CARERS AND PROFESSIONALS

I see Asperger Syndrome as a really positive thing. It's been really positive for me – because it has allowed me to turn the world upside down, see it from a totally different perspective.

To me the whole thing of dealing with Asperger Syndrome has opened up a whole new world for me that I would never have seen.

I developed parts of myself I never would have had to. When you have a child with AS you discover your hidden depths and reserves.

For me the positive side of AS is being able to see everything from a totally different perspective and questioning your normal assumptions.

Once you have dealt with AS you don't take anything at face value any more.

AS makes you turn things round and look outside the box.

People are only negative about AS when they don't understand it. As they get to understand it, there's a real admiration for people who live with AS.

I am so in awe of people with AS at times. I mean the challenges that they face on a daily basis. Yet they still maintain a sense of humour most of the time.

So much depends on what is around people with Asperger Syndrome… If they're allowed and enabled to be themselves, then the problems can sometimes be overridden by the advantages.

Aspies need to be with people who understand and encourage them to be themselves.

Imagine if someone had said – this is your future. Here is a picture book to show you your future – I would have said, 'Take your picture book and go away.' No way would I be able to do that. No way would I be able to cope with that. I mean nobody would choose it. But now, having lived with it, and at an age when I can sit and reflect on it, if I could go back in time and had to choose I would say absolutely, I'd never be without it.

If Aspies are allowed and encouraged to develop and grow – what they have to share with those around them is fantastic.

QUOTATIONS FROM PEOPLE WITH AS

The best thing about Asperger Syndrome is you have a unique mindset.

The best thing about me is really my Asperger Syndrome.

A lot of AS people are very strong.

I think you need to be headstrong a lot of the time to achieve things.

Some Aspies are very anxious, very nervous – but despite the anxiety they keep going. That takes great strength.

Media references to AS are unnecessarily negative.

What Asperger Syndrome needs is for someone really famous and successful with AS who comes out and says it. In the same way that, say, the gay community benefited from Freddie Mercury and Elton John.

Knowledge is important for positivity. A lot of standard literature about AS should be rewritten. It contains a lot of the information that is simply not true.

Aspies have a different viewpoint of the world.

Headstong-ness is a good thing.

People with AS generally have some kind of core con-fidence in themselves. For them it's just, 'This is who I am because this is who I am,' and I don't think it's really like that for normal people – because normal people try very hard to conform in a way that AS people don't. The flipside of that is when things go wrong you can't really blame someone else. You can't say it's because I was trying to act like such and such. But the positive side of it is you can look in the mirror and say – this is me, this is not a bad copy of Jimmy down the road!

Parents of people with AS have a very difficult job.

Parents should try to understand the differences between their child and the average child.

Parents should try to understand the differences between themselves and the average person. You see you're not going to get an AS person who has two com-pletely normal run of the mill parents. In my experi-ence there's always gonna be at least one weird one!

Teachers need to understand the difficulties. You know if I was an average person having problems, and if I said look could you give me a hand with this bit of maths cos I'm struggling with it, you would expect the teacher to give me that bit of extra help. It should be exactly the same thing for the difficulties an Aspergers person has. It's part of the teacher's job to help the pupil with difficulties that stop them learning. But that's a part which I think they shun with AS people.

Aspies need to look at the positive side of AS for them-selves.

Aspies can do a lot to help themselves. They need to look at what it is about it they don't like and to be positive they need to work to change that. To be realistic that it's not going to be easy. I mean it's not going to happen overnight. It's going to be a lot of work. It's going to be difficult. And they're going to need all their strength and all their stubbornness to kind of force themselves through this. But it will be worth it in the end.

I'm glad I am an Aspie. It's better than being a sheep or a lemming!

USEFUL WEBSITES

www.asperger-syndrome.me.uk
A website to help families and friends who need some help or support with a child or adult with Asperger Syndrome.

www.aspergerinfo.org/wiredaqtest.htm
Psychologist Simon Baron-Cohen and his colleagues at the Autism Research Centre, Cambridge, have created the Autism-Spectrum Quotient, or AQ, as a measure of the extent of autistic traits in adults. The test is not a means for making a diagnosis but is interesting, nevertheless.

http://aspergers.meetup.com
Meet up with local people affected by Asperger Syndrome for support and discussion.

www.asplanet.info
A website which celebrates and shares all the good, positive and wonderful things about having Asperger Syndrome

www.autism.org.uk/help!
Support for parents and carers of school-age children, young people and adults who have had a recent diagnosis of ASD.

www.bbc.co.uk/headroom/wellbeing/guides/rr_depression.shtml
Find out how you can help yourself or a loved one who is depressed.

www.bbc.co.uk/health/conditions/mental_health.index.shtml
How to maintain a healthy mental ballance.

www.ehow.com/how_2104017_get-support-parents-asperger-children.html
How to get support for parents of Asperger children.

www.kandi.org/aspergers
A directory which can help you find the information you need by
categorising links available for Asperger Syndrome.

www.nas.org.uk
The website of the National Autistic Society.

www.nhs.uk.conditions/Depression/Pages/Questions-to-ask-page.aspx?url=Pa
ges/Questions-to-ask.aspx
Tips from a depression expert.

www.nhs.uk/conditions/Mental-health/Pages/Introduction.aspx?
url=Pages/What-is-it.aspx
General information on mental health.

www.oaasis.co.uk/home
A resource of information and helpline for parents and professionals caring
for children with autism/Asperger Syndrome and other learning disabilities.

www.optimnem.co.uk
Read about the life and achievements of Daniel Tammet.

www.twicegifted.net/id6.html
Individuals with Asperger Syndrome are truly an interesting population.
Gifted individuals with Asperger Syndrome are even more fascinating – and
confusing.

www.udel.edu/bkirby/asperger
Online Asperger Syndrome information and support.

www.wisconsinmedicalsociety.org/savant_syndrome
A link which explores 'savant syndrome' – the juxtapositions of severe
mental handicap and prodigious mental ability.

www.wrongplanet.net
A web community designed for individuals (and parents of those) with autism, Asperger Syndrome, attention deficit hyperactivity disorder, pervasive developmental disorders and other neurological differences.

www.yourlittleprofessor.com
A website devoted to the benefits of Asperger Syndrome, including resources and academic programmes for students with AS.

All websites accessed on 17 November 2008.

BIBLIOGRAPHY

Acworth, B. (1947) *Swift*. London: Eyre & Spottiswoode.

Arshad, M. and Fitzgerald, M. (2004) Did Michelangelo (1475–1564) have high functioning autism? *Journal of Medical Biography 12*, 115–120.

Attwood, T. (1998) *Asperger's Syndrome*. London: Jessica Kingsley Publishers.

Attwood, T., Grandin, T. and Bollick, T. (2006) *Aspergers and Girls*. London: Future Horizons.

Baron-Cohen, S. (2001) *Understanding Other Minds*. Oxford: Oxford University Press.

Baron-Cohen, S. (2003) *The Essential Difference: Men, Women and the Extreme Male Brain*. London: Allan Lane.

Baron-Cohen, S. (2003) *The Essential Difference*. London: Hutchinson.

Boyd, B. (2007) *Asperger Syndrome, the Swan and the Burglar*. Milton Keynes: Authorhouse.

Brian, D. (1996) *Einstein: A Life*. New York: John Wiley.

Cohen, E. (1882) *Lewis Carroll: An Autobiography*. London: Papermac.

Ellman, R. (1979) *Yeats: The Man and The Masks*. London: Penguin.

Fitzgerald, M. (1999) Did Isaac Newton have Asperger Syndrome? *European Child and Adolescence Psychiatry Journal 8*, 204.

Fitzgerald, M. (2004) *Autism and Creativity*. Hove and New York: Brunner-Routledge.

Fitzgerald, M. (2004) *The Genesis of Artistic Creativity*. London: Jessica Kingsley Publishers.

Gardner, H. (1993) *Frames of Mind: The Theory of Multiple Intelligences*. London: Fontana.

Gardner, H. (1997) *Extraordinary Minds: Portraits of Exceptional Individuals and an Examination of our Extraordinariness.* London: Weidenfeld & Nicolson.

Grandin, T. (1995) *Thinking in Pictures – And Other Reports from my Life with Autism.* New York: Doubleday.

Grandin, T. (2005) *The Unwritten Rules of Social Relationships.* London: Future Horizons.

Hackett, P. (ed.) (1989) *The Andy Warhol Diaries.* London: Simon & Schuster.

Hall, K. (2000) *Asperger Syndrome, the Universe and Everything.* London: Jessica Kingsley Publishers.

Hermelin, B. (2001) *Bright Splinters of the Mind.* London: Jessica Kingsley Publishers.

Herschman, D.J. and Lieb, J. (1998) *Manic Depression and Creativity.* Buffalo, NY: Prometheus.

Kolb, A. (1937) *Mozart.* Vienna: Berman-Fisher Verlag.

Lones, J. (1996) Autism and Asperger Syndrome: Implications for Examinations. *Skill Journal 56,* 1996, 21–24.

Lubin, A.J. (1975) *Stranger on the Earth – The Life of Vincent Van Gogh.* St Albans: Palladin.

Maxwell, J.C. (2007) *Talent is Never Enough: Discover the Choices that will Take you Beyond your Talent.* London: Thomas Nelson Publishers.

Monk, R. (1996) *Bertrand Russell – The Spirit of Solitude 1972–1920.* London: Jonathan Cape.

National Autistic Society (2008) *Asperger Syndrome: What is It?* Available at www.nas.org/nas/jsp/polopoly.jsp?d=212. Accessed on 18 December 2008.

Ostwald, P. (1997) *Glenn Gould: The Ecstasy and Tragedy of a Genius.* New York and London: W.M. Norton.

Solomon, M. (1998) *Beethoven.* New York: Schimer Trade Books.

Sowell, T. (2001) *The Einstein Syndrome.* New York: Basic Books.

Sternberg, R.J. and Davidson, J.E. (2005) *Conceptions of Giftedness.* Cambridge: Cambridge University Press.

Storr, A. (1998) *Solitude.* New York: The Free Press.

Summers, S. (2007) *Aspergers – If You Only Knew: A Family's Struggle with Asperger Syndrome.* iuniverse.com

Weeks, D. and James, J. (1997) *Eccentrics.* London: Phoenix.

Wilkie, K. (2004) *The Van Gogh File – The Myth and the Man.* London: Souvenir Press.

Winner, E. (1996) *Gifted Children: Myths and Realities.* New York: Basic Books.

Winter, M. (2003) *Asperger Syndrome: What Teachers Need to Know.* London: Jessica Kingsley Publishers.

Woolf, S. (1995) *Loners: The Life Path of Unusual Children.* London: Routledge.

INDEX